A Long and Winding Beat!

Brian Allinson

ISBN 978-1-5272-8608-5

Contents

Foreword

Brian Allinson has had a remarkable life. He has been, and remains a dedicated public servant following an outstanding career in the police service. His earliest recollections are of unusual circumstances, living with his devoted mother 'below stairs' as she worked, managing to care for him and support them both. Brian had no sense of disadvantage and he flourished in this rural haven as a young child. His childhood and the characters that formed and shaped his outlook are fondly described in his memoir. His early faltering steps, infatuation with Jaguar cars and driving, meeting with Paula, his wife and life-long partner, all seemed to lead him inexorably towards the police service and a career where he ended up at the leading edge of aerial policing.

Early in his police training Brian discovered that the police service dictated even his personal life. He discovered he needed permission to marry Paula and it prescribed even where he should live. In his memoir Brian gives a detailed and important account of life as a constable in the towns of southwest England, when a very basic level of communications technology meant that individual resourcefulness was at a premium. He began his career at a time when a beat officer needed all his wits to cope with the challenges they found on the street. His love of cars was eclipsed in 1978 by his first ever flight in an aeroplane. However, this was not a passenger airplane with all modern conveniences, but a Hawker Hunter jet flown by an exceptional pilot willing to demonstrate aerobatic manoeuvres. The seed was sown, and a passion ignited.

Brian shares with us the humour and the camaraderie with fellow officers that helped him through adversity. There were some aspects of the job that he had to bear alone, and these had an emotional cost. He describes the personal impact of delivering tragic news of a bereavement to families. The diversity of police work is illustrated by his stints on duties ranging from planning and policing royal visits to reinforcing police lines during the miners' strike. His appointment as Chief Inspector and Sub-Divisional Commander at Filton situated him in a place where there was the means to fulfil his desire to develop the use of aircraft in the prevention and detection of crime. Despite budget restrictions he convinced his superiors of the opportunities afforded by police helicopters by demonstrating what they could achieve at the Glastonbury Festival.

In 1995, Brian's dream became a reality as the Western Counties Air Operations Unit was launched. Three years later he reached his retirement age and left the force to embark on his second career. His skills and knowledge were of a premium to companies supplying aircraft to the emerging police air operations across the country and he was soon working for McAlpines and Eurocopter UK. His expertise in aerial policing made him friends from across the world, stretching from the USA to China. The reduction in public spending led to him providing the government with advice in 2011 that would have maintained or improved the efficiency of the proposed National Police Air Service, without reducing the fleet in the way that was planned. Honesty is Brian's trademark, and, in this instance, it cost him his job.

In his memoir he reminds us of how policing has been transformed in his lifetime and his vision about how policing and flight could combine to remarkable effect, has been realised. Retiring for a second time allowed Brian to expand his commitment to public service through his activities as a Councillor culminating in his appointment as Chair of South Gloucestershire Council. Throughout his life he has been a devoted parent and now a grandparent. His memoir will be a treasure for his family and friends and also a wonderful window on policing history for future generations.

Roger Deeks DL

Charlton Musgrove House - Only the cars have changed!

1

My Early Childhood

I was born in February 1945 in Robeston Wathen near Narberth, Pembrokeshire. My father was working for ENSA, the armed services entertainment organisation, and I understand that at the time he was working at the nearby RAF Coastal Command base at Pembroke Dock. At some point after I was born, my parents separated, but I was too young to understand that at the time.

My earliest real memories go back to the early 1950s and to a life 'below stairs' in Charlton Musgrove House, a lovely big country house near Wincanton in Somerset.

The house itself had a sweeping drive up to the front door (which of course was not to be used by me). Our access was via a side door, giving access to the scullery, kitchen and living room for the cook housekeeper – my mother. My older sister Jean, was also living with us but as she was nine years older than me she had started work and rode her bicycle into Wincanton each day.

Despite, our somewhat lowly position in the household, it was a very happy time in my life. The owners of the house, Major and Mrs Davie, were lovely people and treated mother and myself with great consideration. I was often allowed to play with their two children Simon and Lavender. Simon was about ten then, and Lavender was about my age, six years old.

As cook housekeeper, Mother was the only real full-time employee/servant in the household, but others such as cleaners and waitresses came in from time to time on the occasions of a big dinner etc. I do remember one special occasion for my mother which happened in the mid 50s: she was issued with a Kenwood Chef food mixer. She was very proud of it, and I believe it was one of the very first to be purchased outside of London.

One thing about being the son of a professional cook was the way that I was brought up to eat food. I was never allowed to show dislike regarding any food that was put before me, only pleasure. On the rare occasion that I really didn't like a particular food, I soon learned that to show any displeasure was the height of bad manners. All food on your plate had to be finished. Such training was to stand me in good stead in future years, for even today, there is no food that I will not eat.

Obviously mother did not have time to prepare separate dishes for me, so I grew up on quite exotic foods. I was used to a cooked breakfast, often kedgeree or braised kidneys on fried bread. No cornflakes for me!

There was one other important member of the staff and that was 'Nanny'. She was a young lady, in her early 20s I believe, employed to look after the education and welfare of Simon and Lavender, but also on occasions me. Major and Mrs Davie, although classed I suppose as 'gentry', were very advanced for the time and certainly did not look down on Mother and I as lowly servants. The only real indication of our position was the fact that our bedrooms were smallish and at the very top of the house, with access via the back stairs rather than the main stairs which I did not use.

Nanny's quarters were on the second floor and included a living room, bedroom and what served as a playroom and classroom.

As was the case with many large houses at the time, Charlton Musgrove House was the central part of a larger estate including a small farm. The farm was worked by 'Prince', or Mr Prince to me. Prince was the cowman, pig man, and general farmhand, who lived in the allocated stockman's house just down the lane. In similar fashion, the house grounds and the kitchen garden were the domain of 'Perry' or again, Mr Perry to me. He and his wife lived in a small cottage on one side of the main farmyard.

I understand that the question of my education initially presented a bit of a problem to the household. At the time of my mother's appointment as cook housekeeper at the house, I was barely over five years old, and not really capable of walking the three miles plus along lonely rural lanes into Wincanton where the nearest school was located. The problem was resolved when Major and Mrs Davie decided that my education should, for the time being at least, be undertaken by Nanny, whose role included the education of Simon and Lavender, until such time as they went to boarding school.

Almost opposite the house was Charlton Musgrove Church. This very old church was the original church of that name. Confusingly however, there was a second Charlton Musgrove Church in another village, also called Charlton Musgrove, about one mile further to the east of the original. I later learned that we lived in the original Charlton Musgrove village, but that after the Black Death, centuries before, which had wiped out many of the original villagers, a second Charlton Musgrove village was then built. Which explains why there are actually two Charlton Musgrove village churches.

It was at the Old Church, whilst part of the church choir, that I was given my first ever responsibility, that of putting out the altar candles. The service of course included the singing of a number of hymns, the last of which was always Lead us heavenly father, lead us, and when the congregation got to the point of singing "Pleasure that can never cloy" in the last verse, it was my signal to stand up, and whilst clutching the long candle snuffer, walk to the altar and put out the candles. I was very proud and enjoyed the task.

One incident that I will never forget happened during a Sunday Service, when Lavender who was sitting in the pews beside me suddenly burst into tears and became quite upset. I was most concerned, and enquired what the matter was. Her reply was, "I don't want to die, I don't want to die." I didn't understand and asked her what had scared her so. She pointed to the engraved tablets of stone, which were on prominent display all around the walls of the church, recording the names of people who had died in the service of their country. She had read it, however, that they had died during the service, and she needed to escape this dangerous place very quickly!

As time went on, Nanny suddenly disappeared, it seemed almost overnight. I never did quite understand at the time, but it eventually transpired, that she enjoyed the occasional night out in town, and as a result was 'in trouble'.

By then Simon and Lavender were away at boarding school during the week, so Nanny was never replaced, and it was time for me to go to the primary school in Wincanton. There were two other children from our small village, so the three of us walked every day on our own, three miles, along the narrow country lanes to school.

We walked every day, whatever the weather. Today that may seem very harsh when judged against modern standards, but remember that then, in the early 1950s, very few ordinary people had cars, and there was almost no school transport available. Major Davie had a big Humber Super Snipe motorcar, which I did have ride in very occasionally, but never to school.

When we first arrived at Charlton Musgrove I was quite lonely to start with. I had almost no one to play and mix with. Luckily, the Major and his wife were quite modern, from a social class point of view, and certainly never prevented me from mixing with Simon and Lavender when they were around. However, there were other opportunities to meet local children, mainly on Sundays at the church service.

The stockman 'Prince' had two daughters, the youngest one had spina bifida, the eldest was about my age but had different interests from me (dolls!). Another farm a short way away also only had girls to play with. Toys were very basic – a ball, a cap gun and a pocket knife. Simon had some lovely toys including a Mamod steam engine that we sometimes got going. It had a burner which you filled with methylated spirit, lit and placed under the boiler which of course was filled with water. Soon the flywheel was whizzing around and you could then power up some additional accessories using the belt-driven flywheel on the side of the steam engine.

For my 6th birthday, one of the cowmen from Lower Church farm just down the lane, made me a toy farm. It was on a square plywood base and had fields, hedges and lanes painted onto it. It even included farmyard buildings. He and his wife also gave me a few plastic cows, horses and pigs to put on it. I loved it, and over the next 18 months or so my stock of plastic farm animals grew and grew.

It might be difficult to imagine today, but in those days I had never seen a television! They had actually been invented a short time before the war, but were very expensive and even by the early 1950s, very few ordinary people had them. The best we had for entertainment then was a radio in our sitting room, and I can remember listening to it some evenings. For a seven-year-old it wasn't very exciting, although there was one new station, Radio Luxembourg, which seemed a bit better, but it wasn't very clear and kept fading away. Later I listened to 'Journey into Space' and 'Dick Barton Special Agent' – they were very exciting but a bit scary too.

Then one day we heard that Mr Prince had got a television, and we all went down to his cottage to see it. There was only one channel in those days, and the picture was only black and white of course, as colour had not yet been invented. Most of the time it was only showing a test card, as the actual television programmes were only transmitted for a few hours each day and usually started with the news at teatime. The news was always read by a gentleman wearing a dark suit and a tie and it seemed that there wasn't much that I was interested in. There were a few children's programmes shown each week, Watch with Mother and Muffin the Mule were popular but I didn't like them much, as they were too young even for me. What would really surprise people today was the small size of those early television screens, many were as small as eight inches, but most were about ten inches. The wooden cabinets they were in, however, were quite substantial.

For most people, the real excitement came in 1952 when we heard that the Queen was going to be crowned at her Coronation and for the first time it was going to be shown on the television. (It wasn't really called TV in those days.)

On the day of the Coronation everyone from all the houses and farms around gathered at Mr Prince's house, and we all watched it together. There were a great many of us all crushed into his living room. I really didn't understand much of the ceremony, but liked watching all the soldiers and horses. Everyone was very happy and we had cakes and orange squash. The grown-ups had some beer!

Sometimes the church would organise days out for local people and their children. A favourite destination was Weymouth in Dorset, about 40 miles away. A coach, usually a Bedford OB seating about 25, would tour around the area visiting the villages and then, when full, head off through Sherborne and over the Dorset hills to Weymouth, arriving in the late morning. We would spend a lovely day on the beach, watching the Punch and Judy show and having an ice cream. Sadly, our actual time at the seaside tended to be quite short, because at about 4.30 we all had to be back on the coach for the long slow journey back home and the boring circuit around the villages dropping everyone off. Again, very few cars in those days so the coaches had to stop at every village.

Another much closer and much loved destination for us was the Penselwood area, including Stourton Tower, otherwise known as King Alfred's Tower, where it was said that King Alfred burned some cakes whilst hiding from Viking marauders.

That area, on the border with Wiltshire and Dorset, also had many other attractions such as Stourton Gardens and Shearwater lake, where I first learned to swim. At first we had to rely on someone providing some sort of transport to take us there, but later when we learned to ride bikes, the closer spots like King Alfred's Tower came within an easier self-propelled range. I loved playing in those woods near the Tower. I found the Tower really exciting, but we couldn't get inside, it was all sealed up. It was explained that a few years before, during the war, an English bomber returning from a raid had clipped the top before crashing in the woods nearby. Today the Tower is managed by the National Trust and has been repaired and recently, for the first time ever, I climbed to the top. What a view!

Wincanton Primary School in those days was quite basic. I remember that our teacher was very kind, but she could also be very strict. Mrs Edwards, or 'Miss' to us, was certainly not young, well not when compared to Nanny anyway! Every day we were expected to drink a third of a pint of milk, which was supplied in small glass milk bottles. These bottles often froze solid in the winter, and the foil cap would rise up on a column of frozen milk. We used to de-freeze them around the only form of heating that we had, a large round black coke stove, which sat on its four legs in the middle of the classroom. It used to glow very hot sometimes, and Mrs Edwards was obviously worried that we might burn ourselves. It smelt a bit too. It wasn't very efficient, so on the coldest days we would keep our coats on during lessons.

We learned to write using pencils, but after a while moved on to very basic pens – just a wooden stem with a brass or bright metal nib at one end – which we dipped into ink in order to write. So there was one extra task that we had to perform in those days, which children today would not recognise: we used to take it in turns each week to be the 'ink monitor' and fill all the ink wells that were provided on each desk.

As I got a little older and made friends at school with other boys from Wincanton, Bayford and Templecombe, our area of exploration grew and grew. Our bikes were essential. Today the freedom we had then, to roam all over the area, would seem risky to modern parents but then there was almost no traffic on the roads, and the traffic that was around was slower moving and much noisier than now, so you got out of the way.

Apart from the need to explore, we were also driven by an urgent need to find suitable spots to carry out the important task of train spotting – collecting train numbers and marking them off in our 'Ian Allen' reference books.

The summer months were lovely, and I spent many long days ranging over the fields and brooks between Charlton Musgrove House and Bayford where I had many friends from school. To get to Bayford I had to cross the small but quite shallow River Brue. That was a great place to play too.

Wincanton Racecourse was also a main attraction for me, not for the racecourse itself, but the fact that it required a staff of grooms for the horses and people to maintain the course itself. They lived in cottages nearby and had children of my age to play with. We would usually play war games – English against the Germans! Lots of noise shrieking and supposed gunfire was the order of the day.

By then my sister Jean had moved down to Dartmouth and had started work as a receptionist at the Royal Castle Hotel in the centre of the town.

I had now progressed to the junior school and had obtained a set of roller skates. I would ride my bike to school, put it in the bike racks and then join the others racing around the playground on my roller skates. They were very popular, but were also very noisy in those days because they had metal wheels. Rubber wheels came along quite a bit later.

As we got older, our walk to school got more interesting. For example, at the foot of Racecourse Hill was a small garage. Really nothing more than a corrugated tin shack, but it was the local source of Jowett cars. There you might see Jowett Bradford vans, or the very advanced (for its day) Jowett Javelin car. Yes, my interest in things mechanical was already awakening.

But by early 1958 my life below stairs would be coming to an end. Mum was getting older and she said it was time to move to Yeovil and start a new chapter in our lives. She wanted to retire from the hard life of being a cook housekeeper.

So I had to leave Wincanton Junior School where I had spent many happy times. Even today I look back on my days at the school with much gratitude, especially towards Mrs Edwards, who spent a great deal of her time encouraging me to read confidently and to enjoy books.

Yeovil Tech School

2

Teen Years and Yeovil Technical School

Leaving the slow pace of life in Charlton Musgrove and moving to Yeovil was initially a very traumatic period for me. For at the same time my father came back into our lives. Mother and he had separated well before our move to Charlton Musgrove House, and so I had really grown up without him being around. Now he was working as a bus driver at the big Southern National bus company depot in Yeovil.

We had moved into a brand new but quite small terraced council house in Monmouth Road, Yeovil. The development, on the extreme eastern edge of Yeovil town, was so new that Monmouth Road itself was as yet unsurfaced. All the homes in the area were similarly newly built.

I remember too, the hardships that we put up with for the first few months at Monmouth Road. All of the furniture that we had used at Charlton Musgrove House had belonged to Major and Mrs Davie, so that when we moved into Monmouth Road we didn't have much. I remember Mum and Dad sitting on seaside-type deckchairs at first and that the bedrooms were quite basic. Again there was no television, but we did have a radio. Eating had changed a lot too and I was getting used to a lot of baked beans and tinned spaghetti which I thought was horrible. Mum was still a good cook though, and when we could afford it, she did wonderful things with eggs.

Opposite the house were open fields and a very muddy pond surrounded by trees and scrub. It was a great place to play and develop friendships with people of my own age who lived close by. A very different situation to that which I had grown used to in Charlton Musgrove.

Another big change for me was my new school, a big secondary modern school called Grass Royal. It was quite frightening at first because of course I had only experienced much smaller schools, like the one in Wincanton which had a total school population of around 80 to 100, and quite small class sizes.

In contrast, Grass Royal had at least six times that number of pupils, spread over four year groups. Each year was then also split into three further class groups, dependent upon the academic attainment skills of the pupils. It was evident that my earlier schooling at Wincanton had been of a good standard because I was allocated a place in the top class group for my year.

There was still very little car ownership by ordinary families at that time, so we all either walked or rode our bikes to school. I don't recall anyone being driven to school or even arriving by school bus.

For me, Grass Royal was a good school and opened up some interesting new subjects for me. We learned French (or tried to) and we also had music and drama classes.

Once the initial shock at the change of pace wore off I began to really enjoy my time at Grass Royal. However, quite suddenly it was time to sit the 13+ examinations, which provided an opportunity to move on to a grammar school education. (Even today I don't recall ever taking the 11+ which presumably I must have failed.)

A few weeks later, I learned that I had passed the 13+ and was to be interviewed regarding which school I was now to be sent to. The interview took place within a fairly short time and I was subsequently allocated a place, not at the grammar school as had been expected, but at the secondary technical school situated much closer to the centre of Yeovil.

'Yeovil Tech' was another new experience all together! Firstly, it was an all boys school and in contrast to the relatively newly built complex that was Grass Royal, Yeovil Tech was spread over a number of Victorian, fairly run down buildings. The main assembly room, for example, had the floor and desks raised cinema-style, the further back you were seated, the teacher having a clear and unobstructed view of his class. As its name suggested, it specialised in teaching technical and engineering subjects, to the detriment of any of the arts. And unlike Grass Royal which had a fairly relaxed discipline regime, discipline at the Tech was very strict and rigidly enforced.

The 'Tech' also introduced another new experience to me, that of wearing uniform. The mandatory uniform consisted of black or navy blue trousers, a black blazer with light-blue piping around all edges and pockets, white shirt, school tie and school cap, which again was quartered black and light blue.

The full uniform was to be worn at all times during the school day, including on public transport to and from school. To be seen on a bus whilst not wearing your cap was to risk having to write several hundred lines of 'I must wear my cap on the bus' after school that day.

Lessons included the usual Maths and English, but now introduced Algebra, Geometry, Physics, Technical Drawing, Workshop Theory and Practice, Building Construction, Woodwork and Physical Training (PT). The only soft subjects taught were Geography and History. Class sizes were relatively small at roughly 14 boys.

As indicated earlier, discipline was very much a factor and was enforced firmly. To be caught talking in class risked having to duck quickly as a heavy blackboard rubber whizzed your way. Any failure to comply with the rules would result in a very painful visit to see the headmaster!

Nevertheless, it was a great school to be part of, and the spirit of camaraderie amongst the boys was excellent. Wednesday afternoons were devoted to sporting activities, usually football and cricket, dependent on the season, but occasionally cross country running was an option, introduced to build up stamina.

Much emphasis was made on the importance of passing your GCEs by the time you left school, and so increasingly we were sitting mock examinations, taking previous years examination papers for our questions.

In the last six months of our schooling we were not only being pressed by the need to pass the exams looming ahead of us, but also now the equally important subject of having a job to go to. The idea of our not having an already settled future employment, was something our class teachers or the headmaster would countenance.

My love of cars, especially the quick ones, had caused me to make my way to the local Jaguar dealer in Yeovil, W. Sparrow & Sons, where I enquired if they had any jobs suitable for a 16-year-old. They appeared to like my initiative and agreed to take me on, once I left school. So that was settled. Now for those GCEs!

My studies paid off because ultimately I left Yeovil Tech with good GCE grades in Maths, English, Physics, History, Technical Drawing and Engineering Workshop Theory and Practice. In my final year, I had been appointed head boy and senior prefect. I was even allowed to issue the most basic punishment to miscreants, that of writing lines. My final school report was very good and would stand me in good stead later.

Sadly, that great school was never to survive the move to comprehensive education that came along a few years later. It was closed and demolished. A big new general hospital was built on the site and today there is no sign of the great times that I had there.

My last day at the Tech ended in a big party at the school one Friday in July 1961. We said our goodbyes to our friends, many of whom we would not see again. The Tech being a somewhat specialised school had taken pupils from all over Somerset, and so in many cases it was unlikely that we would bump into our friends again.

Jaguar Mk 2 | © Jaguar Heritage Trust

3

First Job

W. Sparrow & Sons,
Yeovil

I had been told that it was important that I should start my working life immediately on leaving school, and so on the very next Monday I found myself reporting to Sparrow's garage in Sherborne Road, Yeovil. I had been found a job as the clerk in the 'Cost Office'. My working hours were 8.30 am to 5.30 pm each working day, plus 8.30 am to 1 pm on Saturdays. A lunch break between 1 and 2 pm was allowed, but was unpaid. This all amounted to a 44.5 -hour week, for which I was to be paid the princely sum of £3/14s/7d per week, or just under £3.75 in today's money. However, to my dismay tax and stamp etc. brought my take-home pay packet down to £2/18/1d (£2.90). I certainly did not feel rich.

What did come as a much worse shock however, was the massive increase in my hours of work each day. School had started at 9 am and usually finished by 3.45 pm at the latest. So the nearly three hours per day extra, plus the four and a half hours each Saturday, came as quite a shock to the system.

The garage itself was the main dealer in the area for Jaguar, Triumph and Singer cars. There was quite a large showroom immediately to the right as you walked in through the main entrance, Offices to the left, and to the rear were the workshops. The building was quite old, and certainly not well lit, as are garages today. However, what was clearly a big problem then and was never resolved were the stout brick supports that existed almost every ten yards or so to support the roof. New cars in the showroom were squeezed in around them, but it was even more of a problem for the mechanics in the workshops who were constantly having to move cars about as they were serviced.

My job was to examine each mechanic's daily job card, on which they gave brief details of work done on each car and the hours and minutes that they spent working on each one. The hours worked were then added to the job card which existed for each car being worked on. At the conclusion of the work being carried out, I would then provide the senior clerk with the complete picture of the hours worked on the car plus the cost of any spare parts or oils used. From that the bill was prepared. A very complicated but quite accurate method of recording the work done.

The two bosses at Sparrows were Mike Fitzgerald, an ex-RN Lieutenant Commander, and Pat Shirley, an ex-RAF Squadron Leader from 617 Sqn. He had a tendency to drive very quickly and the guys in the garage referred to going flying with Pat rather than driving. However, for all practical purposes my real boss was the service manager Harold Pearson. Harold ran those workshops with a rod of iron. Obviously a skilled mechanic in his own right, he watched over the activities of his team of mechanics closely and ensured that the apprentices learned their trade properly.

But for me, the real stars of the job were the cars! I could sit in Jaguars and smell the leather. I could marvel at all the instruments and dream of the day when I could drive one. Then there were the Triumph Sports cars – the TR3As and of course the Triumph Herald 1200 which I suppose was the bread and butter of the garage at the time. We also sold and serviced Singer cars. Singers were the posh versions of the Hillman cars, such as the Hillman Minx. Our equivalent was the Singer Gazelle. They were built by the Roots Group.

Harold Pearson made it very clear that whilst I was not going to enter an apprenticeship to become a mechanic, he believed that I would perform my administrative role much better if I mixed with the mechanics, watched them working and understood the basics of their work. That wise decision did ensure a much better understanding of my role and assisted my progression towards other responsibilities in the garage later.

The mechanics, about a dozen of them, ranged across a very wide skills base. The top man was Bill Dufty a skilled Jaguar mechanic, who could be relied upon to carry out any task on those powerful machines. He had a small group of less well-experienced men working with him and at least two apprentices. Then came the Triumph team and then the Singer guys. They were used to working on all of the Roots group vehicles.

At first the mechanics treated me with great suspicion but as my enthusiasm and knowledge grew so did their trust and helpfulness. But there was one occasion right at the start when my mischievous nature risked all. It came about during a tea break when it had been decided by the mechanics that I, as the most junior person in the garage, should make the tea for them. There was a big tea urn in the canteen. I protested that I wasn't a mechanic or an apprentice and anyway I didn't drink tea. I had a flask of coffee in the office.

Harold stayed out of that one, watching developments. Eventually, I very reluctantly agreed to make the tea. I filled the urn with water and switched on the electricity. When it got quite hot (but way off boiling) I threw in some tea and then some milk and retired back to the office quickly. There was soon a great commotion from the canteen and then a lynch party came looking for me. It took a bit of ducking and diving but they eventually saw the funny side and left me alone. They never asked me to make the tea again!

As the months went on, I got more and more involved in the day-to-day work of the garage and gradually learned through familiarity, the basics of driving. Even more importantly, I learned the skill of manoeuvring the cars in tight spaces around those brick supporting pillars. Then on the 1st February 1962 I became 17 and was able to learn to drive a car legally on public roads. It was obvious that the garage management expected me to pass my test at the earliest opportunity.

There was a driving school attached to Sparrow's Garage. It was owned and managed by Mr and Mrs Stock, and made use of a Triumph Herald 1200 car supplied by the garage. So it was to them that I turned to teach me properly and prepare me for the test. It was quite expensive for me, still on quite a low wage. Even at discounted rates it cost about 10 shillings (50p) an hour to learn. But it was worth it, for three weeks later I passed my test at the first attempt. Now the real enjoyment of working in the garage would start!

My position in the cost office was immediately behind the service manager's cabin, so I was at hand if someone was required to fetch or deliver a customer's car. My experience of different cars and their peculiarities grew very rapidly. Some cars like the Old Standard Vanguards had a column gear change which was new to me, and worse still had a peculiar curved, almost banana-shaped, handbrake under the right side of the dashboard. However the ones that you had to watch carefully were the Mark One Jaguar saloons.

The Jaguar car company had introduced their 2.4 litre saloon in 1955 and a while later they added the 3.4 litre version to the range. The earlier versions had drum brakes fitted, but as racing experience had shown the effectiveness of the new fangled disc brakes, all Jaguars had been fitted with discs since about 1957. However, the problem was that in those early days no one had realised that disc brakes resulted in very ineffective handbrakes!

Thousands of owners of Jaguar Mk 1 saloons were finding that after they set their handbrakes and got out of their car, the car then had a tendency to follow them as they walked down the road. Until the problem could be fixed, it was essential to leave them in gear, or turn the wheels into the kerb to have any chance of securing your car. A modification was quickly brought out! By the time I arrived at Sparrow's Garage, the beautiful new Jaguar Mk 2 saloon was out, and how I loved them, especially the 3.8 litre version. It drank petrol at about 14mpg but at 5 shillings (25p) per gallon, who cared?

Soon I was being used regularly to catch the train to Taunton, about 32 miles away, to collect new Triumphs and drive them on their first journey to Sparrow's' Garage in Yeovil. Most of the Triumph Herald 1200s, and later the very powerful Triumph Vitesse 6 saloons sold in the region, were first driven by me. However, the most exciting were the Triumph TR4s and later TR4A sports cars.

Also in 1963, there occurred a development that was eventually to have a very important influence on my future life, and that of my family. For I had noticed a very trim and smart young lady that walked past the garage entrance every day. She usually wore a cream-coloured top coat with a green collar. I found her very attractive and decided to ask her out! We seemed to get on very well and within a short time I suppose you could say that we were 'going steady'. Her name was Paula Merrick.

As my driving experience grew, and the management accepted that I could be trusted, I was sometimes required to take a new Jaguar to another dealer and swap it for another Jaguar of a different colour, as wanted by our customer. By the time I was 19, I was often driving new Jaguars all over the country on such exchanges. On rare occasions too, they were the brand new E-Type sports cars.

I just loved my job!

Things were to get even better very soon. Our combination of Jaguar cars plus Triumph and Singer, was a good one, and it was evident that Sparrow's was doing well. The sales department was under pressure and when I became 19 in 1964, Pat Shirley my boss, and John Mead the sales manager asked me if I would like a move from the cost office to the sales department. There would be a pay rise, and better still an opportunity to earn commission. I accepted very quickly!

But I now had to learn a whole new set of skills. And here the service manager Harold Pearson was going to be the key. For I now had to learn how to present a car during a demonstration drive, in order to bring out its smoothness, stability and control. But this was not all about speed. The Jaguar catchphrase at the time was 'Grace, Pace, and Space' and I had to be able to impress on prospective buyers those qualities. But that ability also applied to all the other cars that we sold, both new and second hand.

However, the most vital skill that I had to learn was how to evaluate effectively the cars that I was buying in by way of part exchange. Harold went to great pains to teach me how to listen to what every car that I evaluated was telling me. I learned how to relate all sounds, smoke and smells that were not normal, to the expenditure required in order to be able to confidently resell that car on to any new buyer.

It was drummed into me that this part of my task of being a salesman was not only vital to Sparrow's reputation as a garage, but to my success and continued existence as a salesman. Each deal that I made was down to me. I was the one that agreed the trade-in value of the customer's car. Not the sales manager as happens today. The sales manager was ultimately in charge of the sales department, and would very quickly come down on me if I were giving unrealistic valuations. But it was me in the first instance that agreed the price allowed.

Another practice that was common then (and was very different to normal practice today) is that we retained, for sale on our forecourt, all cars that we took in as part exchanges. That was another factor that made it essential that my buy-ins were properly valued.

Modern motorists would be amazed at the prices that cars attracted in the mid sixties. For example, a new Triumph Herald 1200 was £647, including two essential extras – the heater and front disc brakes. A brand new Triumph 2000 saloon which had only just come on the market was £1,115. None of the cars then were fitted with such luxuries as a radio. Once again they were extra. I could put a new Jaguar Mk2 2.4 litre on the road for a little under £2,000, but an E-Type would cost you around £3,000.

I had grown used to all of the Jaguar sports cars. The iconic Jaguar XK 120 was still around then, and I had driven several of them. The XK140 was much better, and I really loved that car, but for me the best of the best will always be the stupendous XK150S.

The Jaguar XK150S was fitted with the fantastic 3.8 litre XK engine from the Mk 2 saloon, but was much improved in the 150S by being fitted with triple SU carburettors. Somehow for me that wonderful XK150 just seemed to outclass even the more famous E-Type sports that followed.

When it was introduced, the E-Type of course was one of the wonders of the motoring world. People would come in just to look in awe. It was so different! People wondered at the magnificent gleaming 3.8 litre twin overhead camshaft engine fitted with no less than three big SU carburettors. The SUs were generally accepted as being the best carburettors available, but apart from the XK150S, no other car had three of them. This car even had three windscreen wipers.

Remember that not very many years before quite a few cars were sold whereby the passenger visor and passenger windscreen wiper were extras!

I remember even today, that first three E-Types that I sold all had accidents at the end of their first day with their new owner. You see, the E-Type was the first really streamlined car that was offered for sale in the UK. So aerodynamically perfect was it, that the bonnet profile flowed down to the oval air intake at the very front. This meant that whilst sitting in the driver's seat, you simply could not see the first few feet of the bonnet.

We had always warned new owners of that fact, but they immediately fell so much in love with their new possession that they promptly forgot about our warnings, and parked their new car through the end wall of their garage when they got home! Sadly a new E-Type bonnet would cost about the same as a new Triumph Herald 1200.

My career in the sales department introduced me to some lovely people. Every year I would call to see a prominent farmer, Jim Clothier at Wyke Champflower near Bruton. I would be demonstrating the latest Jaguar saloon. Each time Jim bought a new car, his one-year-old car was then passed to his son and it would be the two-year-old car that I would be buying back in.

We both knew that at the end of the day he would buy the car I was demonstrating, but it would always take me the whole of the day to finally close the sale. Jim was a typical old school farmer, and he expected to argue for hours regarding the cost to make the change. I would walk out at least twice, be called back and then thrown out several times too.

The argument would last over lunch and then continue until about 4 pm when we would finally agree on a figure to change! That charade was part of the game and we both looked forward to our annual tussle.

Jim told me years later, when I called on him to say goodbye, on leaving the motor trade, that the reason he always bought from me was the respect that he had for our annual battle.

One of the services we would offer to our customers was a collection and delivery service, at least for a couple of years after the initial sale! Little did I know it, but one day that quality service was to result in me being arrested for stealing a car! (But it's not quite how it sounds!)

In the first instance, I had sold a new Triumph Vitesse 6 to a customer living not far from Yeovil. I had taken back in part exchange his blue and white Triumph Herald 1200, which was now in our possession. However, he had been a customer who made use of a personalised number plate, which of course had now been transferred to his new car.

Coincidently, a few weeks earlier I had sold a Singer Vogue car to a lady living in Bridport who now wanted me to collect her car and bring it back to our garage for its first service. I obviously needed transport to get to Bridport, so it was agreed that I would use the traded-in Herald 1200 which had not yet been cleaned and readied for sale. Its number plates had been removed so to be able to drive it legally on the road, we put on our general trade plates, which all garages used.

At 6 am the next day I set off for Bridport driving the Herald. What none of us knew then, was that on the previous evening a blue and white Triumph Herald identical to the one I was now driving, had been stolen during a burglary in Dorset.

As I neared Bridport, I became aware of a large Wolseley police car following me quite closely. But I wasn't worried, after all I hadn't done anything wrong and certainly hadn't been speeding! However, quite suddenly as I rounded a bend just as I got to Bridport, there was a roadblock ahead which forced me to stop. Before I knew what was happening, my driver's door was wrenched open, I was dragged out and very quickly found myself being thrown into a cell in Bridport police station. I was told that I had been arrested on suspicion of stealing a motor car – the one that I had been driving – and possibly robbery as well.

It was not yet 7 am so my explanation regarding why I was in possession of a very similar car to one stolen in Dorset, and which had clearly had its registration plates removed very recently, could not be verified until Sparrow's Garage opened at about 8.15 am. So I spent a very frustrating period sitting in that cell in Bridport. Eventually, of course, the garage opened and my story was confirmed! I was taken out, dusted down and sent on my way! They didn't seem very sorry, more annoyed that the arrest was refused.

My father had started a business promoting football pools and it quite rapidly became a full-time occupation for him. He stopped driving the buses and opened a small office in Yeovil. At the same time, we moved away from the very small house in Monmouth Road and moved into a larger detached house in Goldcroft Road. Sadly, within a few years his health was obviously failing, and he underwent a serious operation in

Yeovil Hospital. He was suffering from colon cancer and the prognosis was not good. Despite further treatment and a second operation, he died a couple of years later.

By early 1968 I was getting a little unsettled with my life in the motor trade. I loved the excitement of being able to sell and drive some lovely motor cars but I needed something more. I needed a real career which offered a decent future and a proper path to greater things. Ideally I was looking towards the armed services, preferably the Royal Navy, but there were serious difficulties which now combined to make that unlikely.

My father's death had left us unable to keep our home in Goldcroft as a viable proposition. There had been no equity in his business and my earnings were not sufficient to take over the mortgage on the house. My sister Jean had met Stan a serving Naval Petty Officer also from Yeovil originally, and they had married and were now living in Cowplain, Hampshire, near the Portsmouth naval base. Effectively, therefore, I was now the only breadwinner in the family. Leaving mother on her own in order to join the forces was really not possible. In addition, I was still seeing Paula on an almost daily basis and that also made moving away far less attractive. So I resolved to continue at W. Sparrow & Sons, a job that I still enjoyed.

Then, as so often happens in life, a chance meeting was to change everything.

I had been working in the garage one Saturday as usual, when I saw a smart looking gentleman showing interest in a used Rover 2000TC that we had in our showroom. I went over to speak to him and it was clear that the Rover 2000TC was the car he had been looking for.

I took him out on a demonstration road test and he subsequently decided to buy the car. It was during our many conversations over that period that he recognised my frustration at not being able to join the services. He then revealed that he was in fact the Chief Superintendent of Police in Yeovil, George Matthews, and he suggested that I should consider a career in the police service. This was something I had not previously considered, but the more that I thought about it, the more I realised that it did offer the varied life and structured career path that I sought. My application went in soon after!

At about the same time, Paula and I decided that it was high time that we got engaged to be married, and so those plans were formerly announced to our many friends and family members in Yeovil.

Very Young PC1002

4

A Career
in Policing

My application to join the Somerset and Bath Constabulary was acknowledged by letter giving notice that I was to be called for an interview at the force training centre at Cannonsgrove just outside Taunton. The letter confirmed that my GCE O level passes were sufficient not to have to sit the normal police entrance examination.

So in late August 1968 I found myself sitting before a formidable panel of three very senior police officers who were clearly determined to give me a very hard time! I had done my homework and had spoken to a number of serving officers, all of whom had warned me of the pressure that I would be subjected to during this interview and they were correct.

This first of two interviews lasted about 40 minutes that morning, and each of the three senior officers took turns in questioning my motives for wanting to join, my honesty and integrity, and my determination not to back down. It was quite a shock initially, despite the warnings I had received, but after a while I actually began to quite enjoy the exchange. Then as the interview progressed, I think that they realised that I was not going to be discouraged or give in to their bullying tactics.

There then followed medical examinations and fitness tests prior to a second interview in the afternoon. That second interview was very different to the earlier one, and was more concerned with looking into my awareness of current affairs, my sporting and leisure interests and general approach to life. I was then told to sit outside whilst my application was considered.

Finally I was called back in, and offered the position of being a probationary police constable in the Somerset and Bath Constabulary. I accepted with great delight.

And so on the 14th October 1968 I reported as instructed, back to Cannonsgrove, where my initial two-week induction course commenced. I was allocated my 'collar number', No 1002. That collar number would stay as my personal identification number throughout the 30 years of my service.

The term 'collar number' stems from the early days of policing when officers wore tunics which featured stiff high collars. They wore prominent numbers on those collars in order that they might easily be identified. Even today, the collar number remains as an integral part of an officer's uniform. However, they now appear either on shoulder epaulettes or another prominent position.

During that initial induction course lasting two weeks, we were issued with our uniforms. The issue comprised of two thick winter weight, lined tunics with trousers to match, and two thinner unlined summer weight tunics and trousers. However, what came as a bit of a shock to me was the fact that the trousers had button flies, something that I had not previously encountered! A greater and even more unpleasant shock was the issue of six bush shirts, for they had separate stiff and starched collars. These separate collars required the use of a collar stud to attach them to the shirt. This was 1968, but the uniform we were issued with appeared to have dated from the 1920s. Finally, our issue was completed by outer clothing in the form of a rain coat, heavy 'trench' coat, and a cloak which we were taught to fold properly in order to carry it over our shoulder when on patrol. Plus, of course, the traditional symbol of the policeman's helmet. We were warned that the helmet must be worn at all times when on duty outside of the police station, including even whilst crossing the yard at the rear of the station in order to reach one of the outbuildings.

Those initial two weeks passed very quickly. We had been issued with several law books, and we were told that we should read and learn the rules contained in them very quickly. At the same time, we were also given a small pocket-sized book containing details of 120 police 'powers and definitions'. This small booklet was to become our Bible, and it was impressed on us that those powers and definitions should be learned by heart immediately, for during the three-month initial training course that we were about to embark on, we would be tested on our knowledge of them almost daily.

Chantmarle

5

The Police District Training Centre,

Chantmarle

The initial three-month training course for male recruits joining all southwest police forces, was located at the Regional Police Training Centre at Chantmarle near Cattistock in Dorset.

Chantmarle itself was a beautiful old manor house, set in its own grounds, with a modern linked dining hall block and kitchens to the rear. Further back again, was what would eventually become a students' accommodation block, but at the time of my arrival in November 1968 was still under the final stages of construction.

At the front of the manor house, the once impressive gardens had been converted to accommodate a formal parade ground. In addition, there was a second smaller parade ground to the rear of the training centre, nearer the partially completed accommodation block. This second parade ground had clearly been laid over what were once large tennis courts.

The actual approach to the training centre was via a narrow lane, which led solely to the centre and also gave access to a car park for students and staff. The park was located in the middle of a group of trees to the east of the main buildings.

We had been briefed to report to Chantmarle by 4 pm at the latest, on the Sunday afternoon immediately prior to the commencement of our course on the Monday.

So at the appointed time and date, I duly presented myself at the training centre, where I was shown to a classroom close to the new accommodation block. There were approximately 20 other new recruits gathered there, and although we were all still dressed in our civilian clothing I learned that we were a mixture of recruits from Bristol, Gloucester, Devon and Cornwall, Dorset, Wiltshire and Somerset and Bath forces. We were all chatting cheerfully when suddenly someone bellowed, "Stand up!" and in marched a grim-faced police sergeant, who then motioned us to sit and proceeded to introduce himself as our class tutor, Sergeant Standley.

For the next hour, Sergeant Standley told us what was expected of us and the way we should conduct ourselves. It all sounded a bit draconian, especially for those of us, the majority, who were not transferring from the armed forces. In future, we would wear full uniform at all times when on the training centre premises and when walking outside we would also wear our police helmets. We would stand to attention whilst addressing or being addressed by a member of the training staff, and when in the classrooms we would stand immediately a member of the training staff entered the room. We would not sit down until directed to do so.

We were advised that each day would commence with a period of drill training on the small parade ground located at the old tennis courts, before marching down in our class squads to the larger formal parade square at the front of the manor house. Once there, a formal inspection would take place, and woe betide us if anyone's appearance was not up to the centre's very high standards.

As if this was not worrying enough, we were then told that we were all now going to have a hair cut! Several of us protested that we had very recently had our hair cut before arriving at the centre, but our protests were ignored and we were marched down to another classroom where all the other first-level students were gathered. The two barbers present then proceeded to cut off almost all of our hair, leaving us with what was then called a 'crew cut'. The floor of the classroom quickly became ankle deep in hair!

Finally, we were taken to our dormitories, located then in the very top of the manor house. We were allocated a bed, sheets, blankets and a wardrobe and left to make our beds. We were advised that on getting up the following morning we should strip our beds, folding sheets and blankets in the approved 'box shape'. The dormitory would then be subject to inspection and if our preparations for the inspection were not satisfactory we would be required to re-make it all again.

Welcome to Chantmarle!

The following morning we were up and having breakfast by 8 am, having already tidied and swept the dormitory and 'boxed our beds'. Then by 8.30 am to the smaller of the two parade grounds for our first drill lesson. This part at least was easy for me, as a few years previously I had joined the Boys Brigade at the Baptist Church in Yeovil, and they had an excellent drill squad which I had been part of.

There were a couple of ex-servicemen in our intake, so the three of us found the drill lesson easy. The same could not be said of the majority however and at least two were dreadful, suffering from what we called 'dolly marching' –they would swing their arms on the same side as their legs, instead of the opposite side. This caused much amusement to the rest of us, and exasperation to the drill instructors.

But at 9 am the relatively easy drill session ended and we were marched down to the big parade ground in front of the manor house and formed up grouped in our classes for inspection.

The inspection did not go well! The deputy commandant marched slowly up and down each of the assembled lines of recruits and pointed to numerous apparent failures in our efforts to press and clean our uniforms and bull our boots in the approved manner. The senior drill instructor, Sergeant George Fernyhough, closely following the deputy commandant, noted down the name of each miscreant in his notebook, barking out an instruction to the recruit to report to his office that evening at 6 o'clock, 7 o'clock and 8 o'clock in full uniform ready for inspection. Such punishment meant that the unfortunate recruit would not be able to relax that evening whilst preparing for the next day's efforts, but instead would be working on ironing and pressing their uniforms, and bulling their boots, ready for even more critical inspection that same evening.

Each morning, that same critical inspection would take place, and it seemed that by the end of the first week just about every one of the junior recruits had been reported for one fault or another. Many of us spent difficult evenings standing outside Sergeant Fernyhough's office waiting for his approval of our turnout. The worst offenders found themselves being appointed duty fire marshals for the coming weekend, which meant that they could not go home as expected, but instead had to remain at Chantmarle making regular security patrols and fire safety inspections.

The next four weeks continued in very much the same manner, with frequent tests on our knowledge of the law and powers of arrest, etc., combined with an increasing number of practical scenarios played out around the grounds of the training centre, depicting simulated car accidents, burglaries and drunken yobs, etc. We were learning how to deal with all manner of offences and situations, often committed by abusive or difficult offenders enthusiastically played by our fellow students.

Our first four weeks on the junior course at the centre were coming to an end and we were just about to go off on our weekend break when Drill Sergeant George Fernyhough entered the classroom. For once he was not so grim-faced and was almost in danger of smiling, but what he said came as a surprise! "Right lads, that's the end of your first four weeks. When you come back on Monday you will be the intermediate class!

When you are inspected on Monday morning, I'm going to pick on several of you for being poorly turned out. I'll shout at you to report to me at 6 and 7 and 8 o'clock, but don't bother, that's just for the benefit of the new junior course, I do like to get their attention. Have a good weekend!"

When we arrived back at Chantmarle the following Sunday night we were surprised to find that we had been allocated our own bed study apartments in the brand new student accommodation now entitled 'Cattistock Block'. Each student now had his own individual room. The rooms were quite small, but it was our own private space, fitted with a single bed, wardrobe and study desk. There was a reading lamp over the desk and a small bedside cabinet and lamp beside the bed. It was pure luxury compared to the dormitories that we had been allocated in the old manor house. True, there were no wash basins in the new rooms – they, together with the showers and toilets, were at the end of the central corridor, meaning that the early morning routine was very much the same as before – but nevertheless it was a huge improvement in the living conditions that we had experienced since we first arrived.

Both the intermediate and later senior stages of the Initial Police Training Course passed by quite quickly. There were frequent tests of our knowledge of law and procedures and ever more practical scenarios. We were also taught how to give evidence in court. These courtroom experiences included how to respond to hostile questioning from defence lawyers.

As the course entered its final few weeks, the most burning question in our minds was, where were we going to be posted? None of us really had any idea, the only thing that we did know was that we would be moving away from our home areas. All the police forces at that time would insist that a new young probationary police constable should learn his duty whilst not hampered or tempted by earlier friends or associates. Home for me was by that stage Yeovil so I knew that I was not going to Yeovil.

The other divisional police stations, where all new probationary constables in the Somerset and Bath Constabulary could be posted, were Taunton, Bridgwater, Frome, Bath and Weston-super-Mare. Of those, I really wanted to be posted to Taunton, a town that I already knew well because of my frequent visits there to collect cars. It was also where the headquarters of the force was located.

At the start of week nine, just as we commenced the final four weeks of the course and were now the senior students, came the brown envelope that we had all been waiting for. I tore mine open and to my relief found that I had been posted to Taunton Division. I was instructed to report to the force's own training school at Cannonsgrove, on the first Monday in January 1969 for a final week of local procedures training, prior to commencing my duties at Taunton Borough.

However, the same envelope contained a memo bearing very worrying news! About two weeks earlier I had met a senior officer from the force who was paying a liaison visit to Chantmarle. During our conversation I had mentioned to him that I was engaged to be married, and that both Paula and I were looking forward to my new career as a police officer. He had not given me any reason to be concerned, but had clearly reported our conversation to the force personnel officer on his return to force headquarters. The memo I now received advised me in no uncertain terms that I was subject to police regulations, and therefore could not marry anyone without the chief constable's permission. Furthermore, no permission would be granted until I had formally submitted a report to the chief constable, through my new divisional commander, giving full details of the woman that I was seeking permission to marry, together with her date of birth, her address and names of her parents and siblings, etc. This caused a certain amount of panic in my mind as we had already set a date for our proposed marriage of the 26th April 1969, only five months from the date of receiving that memo.

Luckily, a friendly Somerset and Bath sergeant at Chantmarle assisted me in the correct form of submitting such a report, and it was submitted without further delay. It may surprise anyone reading this history today, to learn that although this took place in the late 1960s, the police service was still using a report style which went back to the previous century, requiring formal requests such as this to submitted to headquarters using phrases like "Sir, I humbly beg to report that I have been courting a young lady, who is of good character and now seek your permission for us to marry. The lady's name is ...."

Police Initial Training Course no 195 at the Regional Police Training Centre Chantmarle ended with the final parade being inspected by an assistant chief constable from the Wiltshire Force. We then said our goodbyes to fellow course members, with whom we had worked closely together for the past three months. All were now returning to their forces and were looking forward to the real start of their careers. We realised that although we were almost certain to meet our colleagues from our own force again, we were far less likely to see friends from neighbouring forces.

Hillman Imp Panda | © Peter Steel

6

Operational at Last!

Taunton Division

We had Christmas off duty at home. I didn't realise it at the time, but in my case, it was to prove the last time for at least ten years that I would be able to spend the entire Christmas period at home. My force, like all of the others, worked on the principle that you were required to work either Christmas Day or Boxing Day but not both. The same principle applied at New Year.

All of the new Somerset and Bath recruits, wherever they had been posted, were required to attend the local procedures course at Cannonsgrove that first week in January 1969. There we were provided with additional items of uniform to supplement the basic issue allocated before we attended the course at Chantmarle. However, the most significant thing to happen was that we were to meet our allocated tutor constable for the first time.

The tutor constable, was key to ensuring the recruit's future successful career. Each tutor was highly experienced and had been chosen not only for their wide experience, but also their ability to pass on that knowledge to the new recruit. I was extremely lucky, in that my tutor was the very best that the Somerset and Bath Constabulary had at that time. Allan Willoughby was a highly decorated RAF Bomber Command aircrew member who had first joined the police on leaving the RAF after the Second World War. At the time he became my tutor, he had already carried out over 20 years of police service and was a highly respected member of the Taunton Borough Division. He was also the Taunton Division constables' representative on the Police Federation.

My first day actually on Taunton Division passed as a bit of a blur. I had introductory meetings with the chief superintendent and his deputy, and other senior officers. They all appeared quite stern, but Allan was always with me and provided constant reassurance. However, the most important thing now was to meet my sergeant and his section, the group of police constables that I would be working with every day.

I had been allocated to Sergeant Westcott's section, one of four sections policing Taunton Borough. The section comprised of about ten officers of varying ages and experience. There were a couple of experienced men, like Allan Willoughby, and about four officers having between four and eight years' service; but there were at least four probationers with less than two years' service, including myself who of course had no operational experience whatsoever.

In those days, we worked straight shifts of seven days of 10 pm–6 am night shifts (Monday to Sunday), followed by rest days on Monday and Tuesday, then seven late shifts 2 pm–10 pm, rest days Wednesday and Thursday and then early turn 6 am–2 pm Friday to Thursday. Rest days Friday to Sunday before back to nights on the Monday. So we had one free weekend per month. It was also made clear to me that whatever shift I was working on any particular day, I was required to parade for briefing 15 minutes before that shift commenced. The briefing period included details of current crime trends, local stolen cars and other issues that needed to be borne in mind during the forthcoming patrol.

The shifts as described above were quite wearing, especially in my case the early turn one, because to be at the station by 5.45 (at the very latest) meant getting up at 5 am, something I never found easy! Luckily, after a few years it was decided by the chief officers, after talks with the Federation, that the full seven days on each shift was not good for our health. So in order to bring some relief, the early and lates weeks were mixed up a little with no more than three consecutive days on one particular shift. However, the nights week was not altered, and we were always required to perform seven nights consecutively. We had one three-day weekend off duty each month.

I was now classed as a probationary police constable! Police regulations decreed that all police recruits were employed on a probationary basis for the first two years of their service. They would carry out the full duties required of a constable, but their performance and conduct during that period would be closely supervised and reported on. If there was any doubt concerning any aspect of their performance or conduct during that period, then their services could be dispensed with, after suitable warnings were given. In addition, the probationary constable was required to undertake one day's additional training at the force training school per month, in order to maintain their knowledge of law and procedures.

Although I was engaged to be married (my request for permission to get married had not yet been approved), I was still classed as a single man, so had been allocated lodgings with a vetted and approved landlady at a house in Fairfield Road, Taunton. I was required to live there during the working week, although could return to my mother's home in Yeovil on rest days.

On commencing operational duty, the new probationary constable would be accompanied by their tutor constable during the first eight weeks of their service. The tutor would ensure that his student would be exposed to all manner of police duty, from routine patrol and traffic 'point duty' to making arrests and dealing with sudden death, etc.

Allan Willoughby started my settling-in period by introducing me to routine foot patrolling around the streets of Taunton. Not just the shopping area but the back doubles and rear yards of premises as well. I was introduced to shopkeepers and hospital staff, but most importantly I was told where I would be welcome to call in for a cup of tea and where I could leave items of outer clothing if, during my patrols, it got too hot to wear them! Officers were not permitted to return to their station for such unimportant reasons as comfort and convenience once they had commenced their allocated beat.

We dealt with shoplifters, parking offenders and known criminals were identified to me as worthy of 'keeping an eye on'.

Those first few days with Allan were spent working an easy 9–5 routine, but it was not to last and I was soon introduced to the police officers' burden of shift work! We commenced my first ever week of nights carefully guided and advised by my tutor.

Each night, Sergeant Westcott would allocate us a different beat, and in that way I learned all of the important premises and shops on each beat, all of which required careful checking for security each night. I soon learned the dynamics of walking the beat gripping each door handle in turn, twisting and leaning on the door to check if it was locked! Just occasionally a door hadn't been properly secured and you fell inside, often to the sound of the burglar alarm going off! That then required a call on our Pye pocket phone radios to control to call out the key holder. Once again, Allan's knowledge of suitable night-time tea stops was of great importance. The hospital casualty department was an important tea stop and had the extra advantage of providing the vulnerable nursing staff a police presence at least twice during the night.

I made my first ever arrests that week too. The first was very easy, a drunk and incapable man who we had no choice other than to arrest, mainly to ensure his own safety.

The second arrest was much more testing, although in some ways it was quite funny! The subject, 'Tom', was an ex-engineroom stoker on the famous inter-war years liner the Berengaria. Tom, in his 50s, was now shorebound having served, it was said, a period in prison for manslaughter of another seaman in a fight. Tom had turned to the local brew of cider, the rougher the better. The trouble was that Tom drank too much of it, every night, and when he was drunk he wanted a fight!

So one night that week the inevitable happened and whilst Allan and I were crossing a car park there was a loud shout of "What the f******* hell are you b*******s doing here?" Allan sighed and muttered, "I'd better get some back up." He clearly knew that this was going to get interesting. We went over to speak to Tom to warn him about his language, and of course he was having none of it and a fight very quickly started. Tom was a big strong man and the two of us could do little more than try to hang onto him but even that was difficult! Then luckily, a bit like the cavalry coming over the hill, our anti-violence wagon (known as the 'paddy wagon'), driven by Sgt O'Sullivan arrived. The fight got even bigger as about six of us tried to subdue Tom. We finally got him under control and I will never forget Tom, who was by now grinning with a twisted satisfaction singing at the top of his voice, to the tune of 'Raindrops keep falling on my head' except that his version was 'Truncheons keep bouncing off me 'ead'. Another one to sober up in the cells!

I learned quickly at Taunton that there was a particular problem there. It was this. Men who get drunk on beer can get nasty but tire quite quickly. Men who get drunk on cider will fight brick walls! It was an enlightening week.

Our week of nights ended at 6 am on the Monday, technically a rest day, so part of it was spent sleeping. However as soon as I awoke I was away to Mum's small flat in Yeovil where I could relax until Wednesday morning when I had to return to Taunton in order to get ready for my week of 2–10 pm late shifts.

Obviously most of my rest days were spent with my fiancée Paula, planning for our wedding and our subsequent life together. The planned date of our wedding, the 26th April, now seemed very close, yet I still had not received that vital permission from the chief constable to actually get married.

To even have to ask for permission to marry might appear very strange in today's much more permissive society, but the reasoning then was this – the service had spent a great deal of time and money looking into my background before accepting me, and had then further invested a great deal of money in my training. So it was therefore vital, in their minds, to ensure that such expenditure was not endangered by my marrying someone totally unsuitable to be a police officer's wife, by reason of her history or associates!

There was a further restriction that applied then on recruits joining the force which many would find unacceptable today, and that was the restriction on owning property. If you owned a house you could not keep it! Police officers then were required to live in a police house, or if you were a single man like me you had to live in approved lodgings. The reasoning was this, in order to manage his force effectively the chief constable needed to be able to deploy his work force wherever he decided they were needed. To do this he had police houses located near police stations all over the force area and when police officers were posted to a station they were required to live in the house that they were allocated nearby. Regulations stated that married officers could expect a minimum of 14 days' notice of any move of station, and of course house. Single men could expect only 48 hours notice!

At the time of my joining the service, police officers were not allowed to buy their own houses until they had a minimum of 21 years' service, and even then they had to apply for permission.

My continued education into the skills and abilities demanded of a young constable continued on the following Wednesday when Allan and I started the week of 2–10pm late shifts. This late shift was to become my favourite shift, it was usually busy with a wider variety of challenges than the other two shifts offered. Allan taught me how to deal with several different shoplifters during that week and also two thefts from pre-payment gas and electricity meters. That last offence was very common in those days, but almost unknown today. Then, many homes used the pre-payment meters which required being fed with cash, usually a two shilling piece (10p today).

After a while, the meter's locked cash box would contain a great deal of money, the property of the utility, either the gas or electricity company. The presence of that ready supply of money occasionally became too much of a temptation to the householder, who would find some way of breaking the padlock and stealing the money. The theft was usually reported by the meter reader sent to collect the money, or occasionally by the homeowner who then usually blamed some passing burglar who had obviously broken in and robbed the meter. I soon became quite skilled at dealing with both of those very common types of crime.

The late shift often required another skill now not required of the modern police constable, that of traffic control. Taunton in those days had very few traffic lights, but it did by 1969 have quite a few cars and lorries using its streets, especially during the rush hour. We had been taught the basics of traffic control at Chantmarle, but there at best we might be practising with two or perhaps three cars belonging to fellow students. Now I had to learn how to control quite heavy traffic from several different directions, whilst preventing hold-ups from developing wherever possible. You had to be very precise and make your instructions abundantly clear or a nasty accident could occur – with you in a lot of trouble!

The next subject on Allan's list was how to deal with sudden deaths. It was vital that I understood and experienced all the established procedures for dealing with sudden or unexplained death. Never a pleasant experience, it was then, and still is today, a task that all police officers will have to deal with many times during their service.

Whilst dealing with a sudden or unexplained death, the police officer is acting on behalf of the coroner, and must therefore gather any evidence which will assist the coroner to establish the cause of and the circumstances surrounding that death.

It was during that first week of late shifts that I experienced the first of many sudden deaths that I was to deal with during my 30 years of police service. This one proved to be a very sad one indeed.

We had received a radio call to attend an incident at a private school near Taunton. On arrival we were shown to a toilet block on the ground floor where I saw the body of a young boy, apparently aged about 14 or 15. There was a pyjama cord tied tightly around his neck. It had clearly been cut through and we noticed that there was an identical piece of cord tied around a stout water pipe which was located above the toilet area where the body lay. I was clearly dealing with a devastating case of suicide, but the subject person was so young.

The body had been discovered by one of the teachers, who had immediately cut the young boy down, but it was too late. Allan took me through the immediate investigations and interviews with friends and teachers. Senior officers were notified and duly attended, as did the criminal investigation department (the CID), but there were no suspicious circumstances. It was a truly tragic case. Finally, I was instructed to accompany the body to the local morgue in order to provide continuity of evidence.

I will not add any further detail concerning the apparent cause of the tragedy, because although the incident is now about 50 years ago, there might still be family members around. As Allan said later, it was far from being the easy routine example of a first sudden death that his students usually experienced.

I did not sleep easy in my lodgings that night!

Our lates week continued with two more shoplifters and the execution of a number of arrest warrants for non-payment of fines. Finally, we learned that on the last two days of our lates week, Monday and Tuesday, we had been dropped back to a later 6 pm to 2 am shift in order to carry out some observations. Apparently an informant had tipped off the CID that a particular gang of safe breakers were planning to raid some particular premises in the centre of Taunton. The CID had made arrangements for a team of officers to occupy some overlooking offices where we were to set up an observation post.

Accordingly, Allan and myself wearing rough civilian clothing spent a cold and very boring eight hours staring at the rear of a nearby business premises in case somebody tried to break in. To say that it was boring is actually an understatement.

A small team of officers were detailed to carry out the same observations for a further five days but the expected break-in never occurred. It was a clear indication that not all police work was going to be exciting.

I was to find that those early months of being a probationary constable quite often involved a period of shift changes onto observation duties. When such duties were required for whatever reason, supervisory officers were reluctant to take community beat officers or area car drivers off their patch, so it became the normal thing to do, to make use of the less experienced team of town centre beat officers for such tasks. One such operation remains clearly in my mind even today. There had been several hayrick fires on farms in the countryside surrounding Taunton. Initially it had been thought that perhaps the fires had occurred as a result of spontaneous combustion, but it was quite quickly realised that this was the work of a very persistent arsonist.

Now it is a well-known fact that farmers do not tend to be shy retiring types, and they very soon started telephoning the chief constable, Kenneth Steele, to demand action! The chief constable in turn started to give Taunton Division's chief superintendent a hard time and a squad was formed to carry out observations on a minimum of eight vulnerable hayricks every night. I was one of the poor officers selected for this onerous duty, and for quite a long time found myself sitting on a lonely hayrick every night waiting for it to catch fire! There was certainly no chance of you falling asleep, you didn't want to wake up in a fiery furnace!

But we were eventually victorious and caught him! The culprit turned out to be a retained fireman. The rural fire stations, being much less busy than those in the larger towns and cities, relied on part-time firefighters, men who normally carried out ordinary jobs such as mechanics, butchers and shop keepers, but these men were highly trained and prepared to drop whatever they were doing on hearing the fire siren and go off to fight the fire. They received additional pay for turning out in such emergencies. This particular firefighter had decided to supplement his income by setting hayricks on fire, then rushing home and waiting to be called out to put it out. The local magistrates in Taunton did not see the funny side of the matter.

My period of being tutored by Allan passed very quickly, and soon I found myself on patrol on my own. I had every confidence, for Allan had been a first-class tutor, and I had been given a firm base on which to develop my new career.

Despite that confidence, I was still very much the new kid on the block as far as my section was concerned, but without exception my colleagues went out of their way to help and advise whenever I needed guidance. The Pye pocket radio that we all carried was also a great help. Back at the police station, constantly manned was the radio base station operated by a senior and experienced colleague. The main purpose of the radio system was to direct us to incidents etc., but it was a true two-way system, and so we could also use it to call for back-up in case of trouble, or merely to seek advise or directions on a subject that was new to us.

One thing that did annoy me though, was the fact that I was not allowed to drive at all. I was told that it would be at least six months at the very least before I might be allowed to drive one of the Hillman Imp 'panda cars'. And indeed probably much longer than that. I found that restriction exceedingly irksome given my background in the motor trade. But it was the rule and I was in no position to challenge it.

The long awaited permission for me to marry Miss Paula Merrick finally came through at the start of February and I was able to phone Paula with the good news. The permission had taken well over the expected six weeks and we were starting to get quite concerned. However, I had forgotten that the Christmas and New Year breaks would cause additional delay. But now with permission granted, we could really start planning for our wedding day! The church and reception had been booked long ago, but until permission had been granted, we had been unable to make any detailed plans or invitations.

The authority to get married also meant that we needed somewhere to live. The force had a policy that all of their married officers should live in police houses, however due to a recent increase in recruiting there was a critical shortage of vacant police houses.

As a result, I was told I should rent suitable accommodation within the Taunton Division. In addition, the failure to provide me with a police house would mean that I would receive a regulation housing allowance in order to compensate my rental expenses, until such time as I could be allocated a police house. There were a number of approved premises available and as a result we soon found a small ground floor flat in Peter Street, Taunton, that suited our needs.

Obviously, until the date of our actual marriage I was still required to remain at my approved lodgings in Fairfield Road, Taunton. So it was there that I was staying on my last week of night shifts immediately prior to our wedding, when an incident occurred that aptly demonstrates the much firmer level of discipline that applied in those days. I had been working the town centre south foot beat all night, checking the shops and business properties in East Reach. It had been a relatively quiet night and I returned to the station just before 6 am and booked off duty. I got to my digs at about 6.20 and went straight to bed and to sleep.

At about 8.45 am there was a very loud pounding on the front door of my digs and I heard it answered by my landlady. A very gruff voice loudly demanded, "Is Allinson in?" to which my landlady obviously said yes and the voice said, "Get him up, he's wanted down the station."

I was driven to the station by the sergeant that had called at my digs and taken before an inspector who was obviously most displeased!. I was informed that a burglary had occurred on my beat and the inspector was demanding to know how and why I had missed it. I had to submit a duty report, detailing my actions that night and apologising that I had failed to discover the burglary. From my own enquires later on I discovered that the entry had been via an upstairs window reached from the roof of an adjoining building. I could have not seen it even if I had suspected it was happening! No matter, it was on my beat, and I was responsible. Discipline was much stronger in those days.

By now the 26th of April was approaching rapidly, and Paula especially was working very hard to get our flat, No 1 Peter Street, Taunton, ready for our occupation, and brought up to an acceptable standard. It was fairly clean, but old by even the standards of the late 60s. The windows had draughty metal frames and of course no double glazing. Paula bought and made herself all of the curtains and nets. I bought a carpet square big enough to cover most of the sitting room floor. Lino covered the rest. A double bed and some chairs and a table for the sitting room cleaned out all our savings, but we did still manage to rent a black and white 17 inch TV from Radio Rentals!

The worst bit of the flat which we were never able to do anything about was the plumbing. The cold water was OK, even though there was a horrible metal water tank suspended over the pretty small and basic bath. But the hot water system was primitive to say the least! The hot water supply to both the kitchen and bathroom was via separate gas geysers that were not only noisy but smelt and consumed large amounts of gas.

The actual wedding day itself dawned clear and bright and I met my best man, Jerry Fowler, at a pub we both knew well, the Pen Mill Hotel, near Pen Mill station, not far from St Michaels Church where Paula and I were to be married at 1 pm.

The reception was to be held in Sherborne, some eight miles from the church. We had planned we would leave the reception at about 4 pm in order to allow plenty of time to drive down to Torquay where I had booked a room in the Corbyn Head Hotel for the first night of our married life.

Jerry and I had arranged to drive independently to the reception hotel, where I would leave my car, ready for our departure at about 4 pm. Jerry, who I trusted implicitly, promised he would not tell anyone where my car was.

His task now was to drive me back to the Pen Mill Hotel where we were to have a couple of steadying drinks prior to the wedding, and to meet some of our guests and supporters.

We had a great time, but soon after 12.30, Jerry drove me the short distance to St Michaels Church. There, many of our friends and family were already gathering. Paula of course had not yet arrived and I waited nervously with Jerry, hoping that she had not changed her mind. I needn't have worried because suddenly she was there looking absolutely stunning.

The service itself seemed to take such a short time, and almost before we knew it, we were standing outside the church as man and wife. The family photographs seemed to go on for ages, before we were able to drive off to the reception in Sherborne.

The reception was great! Both of our families had always got on very well, and so it was a happy event for everyone. The meal was very good and the speeches not too long. We managed to get around to see everyone, but then our scheduled departure time of 4 pm seemed to arrive very quickly and it was time to say our goodbyes.

We moved towards the front door ready to leave, knowing that my good old Hillman Husky 830 RYD should be waiting outside as arranged with Jerry. It was there alright, but not quite as I had last seen it. It was now covered in sticky tape and ribbons, notices saying 'just married', and several cans and old boots tied to the rear bumper. I could hardly see out of it to drive away!

The drive down to Torquay was otherwise uneventful, and we booked into the Corbyn Head Hotel where we were given a lovely room with a sea view. We decided that the restaurant at the hotel was too expensive even for our honeymoon and Torquay itself looked very inviting. We quickly found a great restaurant and really enjoyed a private meal together, alone at last.

Sadly we could not afford to stay in the Corbyn Head for more than that first night, and so the next morning we drove down to Cornwall and found a small B&B in Falmouth for three nights. We had used virtually all of our savings on the wedding, and also in buying furniture for our flat in Taunton, so this would be quite a short honeymoon. In any event, having only been a police officer for a few months, I had not accrued much annual leave entitlement to be away any longer.

We arrived back in Taunton, on the Wednesday after our wedding, and had a couple more days getting things straight before I returned to work on the Saturday, a week after our wedding.

We settled into our flat quite quickly, and Paula managed to get a job in the Gas Board offices in the centre of town. That certainly helped out with the finances, but more importantly gave her some purpose and direction. It was OK for me working in a strange town, but Paula didn't know anyone in Taunton, and it would have been very easy for her to have felt isolated and alone when I was out working.

We both still remember sitting in the flat one evening in July that year watching the Apollo moon landings on our black and white rented TV. It seemed so futuristic at the time!

At about the same time, further recruitment had meant that I was no longer the most junior member of Sgt Westcott's section. PC 1037 Alan Bailey, had been posted to us and we formed a very firm friendship, Alan was a couple of years younger than me and was married to Penny. Coincidentally, they had also married on the 26th April that year so we immediately had something in common.

Alan was an immensely cheerful and carefree individual, whose tendency to act sometimes without thinking things through could cause chaos, but whatever it was that happened his cheeky and cheerful grin would save the day! But he hated early turn. I remember one week he was late on parade three times, Sergeant Westcott was very cross indeed and made it quite clear to Alan that if he was late again he would go before the chief inspector with a recommendation for the sack.

The next day when I arrived at 5.40 am ready for the early turn briefing, Alan was already there fully dressed and ready for patrol. Sgt Westcott briefed all of us except Alan as to our duties and instructed us to go out on patrol. Alan said, "But you haven't given me a beat Sergeant, what should I do?" The Sergeant looked at Alan and said, "Mmmh, I don't really know Bailey, you obviously haven't looked at the roster, for you are on a rest day today!" We all fell about laughing and even Alan saw the funny side of it!

I had been posted to Taunton Borough sub division, covering the actual county town of Somerset. Taunton Borough sub division was quite a small part of Taunton Division itself. The actual Taunton Division included all the countryside and small towns between the county border with Devon, and the small town of South Petherton, the eastern border with Yeovil Division.

Taunton Borough sub division was policed using the relatively new 'Unit Beat Policing' method of working. The sub division was split into four equally sized areas. Each area was then further split into a small number of unit beats, each beat having an allocated unit beat police constable responsible for it. (The forerunner of what today we call a community constable.) Each of the four areas had a dedicated police 'panda car' providing back-up for the beat officer, and also able to deal with any incident requiring a rapid response.

By this time, I had served operationally for about six months, and I was being teamed up quite frequently with PC 768 Chris Mitchell. Chris was one of the more experienced constables on the section and had about four years' service. He was the area car driver for the no 1 area, on our shift.

It was quite common then for the panda cars to be double crewed on the night shift, when they would often be sent to deal with fights in pubs or domestic disputes, etc. (often some of the most difficult situations that young officers would face). Chris and I made a good team, he was very handy when dealing with violent situations, and I was developing an expertise in dealing with messy road accidents, a duty that Chris didn't like.

The workload of the area cars was increasing all the time. We were expected to serve summonses, execute warrants for arrest, deal with accidents, public order offences and shoplifters. It was non-stop! On top of all that, we were also expected to check vacant houses. In those days, when a householder went on holiday they told the police when they would be away and when they were coming back. We would then be tasked with checking their house for them as often as possible during their absence.

Later that year came the first of the troubles in the Middle East that affected the price and availability of petrol. The price soared up from its normal 5 shillings (25p) per gallon to about 7 shillings! Panic set in, and the chief constable instructed that the panda cars would be limited to 25 miles per eight-hour tour of duty! Yet we were still expected to do all the work that we had been doing before. It just couldn't be done. It seriously affected our morale and we were very unhappy. We took our duties as police officers seriously, and wanted to do a good job.

It was then that my previous experience in the motor trade came to the fore and caused us to do something that was actually against the very law that we were trying to uphold (it's 50 years ago now so I think that I can safely admit it). I had worked on the Hillman Imps in Sparrow's Garage on many an occasion, and I knew that if you put your hand up behind the dashboard you could unscrew the speedo cable and drop it back. The mileometer would no longer record, and we could get on with our tasks without exceeding the allocated 25 miles per tour! Very naughty indeed, but the job was getting done and everyone seemed happy, except for the fleet manager who could not understand why the pandas did not seem as good on fuel consumption as they once were!

But then one day it all went wrong. We were driving through Station Road, Taunton, one afternoon when Chris started sniffing the air and saying, "What's that funny smell?" I said that I had a cold and couldn't smell anything, and then Chris exclaimed "Christ!" and pointed to a thin trace of smoke curling up from behind the dashboard. The end of the speedo cable had touched another terminal and had started to short it out!

Now we had to think quickly! We could either abandon the car and let it burn, or take action to stop the short circuit. The first option was the safest, however the paperwork involved afterwards was likely to be very troublesome indeed! So Chris thrust his not inconsiderable fist up behind the dashboard, grabbed the very hot speedo cable end, and got it away from the electrical circuit that it had come in contact with. The cable soon cooled down enough to reconnect it properly, and we were safe from the dreaded paperwork. All that was now required was a quick visit to the general hospital A&E department for some soothing ointment for Chris's burnt fingers!

The fleet manager was later heard to remark that his Imps were doing much better on fuel again. They must have had a bad batch of fuel!

By early 1970 the increased rate of recruitment into the police service meant that despite the fact that I was still on probation, I was by then one of the more experienced constables on Sgt Westcott's section. However, I was desperately hoping for my turn to be allocated a police house because our flat in Peter Street was cold and not very comfortable. Then one day there was a very official-looking brown envelope in my in-tray. When I opened it I was quite shocked to learn that I was being transferred away from Taunton Borough to the small police station at Ilminster on the A303. But the more important news was that I was being allocated Flat 2 above Ilminster Police Station as my first police house.

Ilminster Police Station was not very old in 1970, and had been built with two large flats above it. The flats had a common stairway up to a small first floor landing in the centre of the building. Flat 1 was located over the front part of the station and Flat 2 the far end of the building. Both flats were the same three-bedroom design, but also offered a large sitting room, a dining room and a reasonably sized kitchen. However, for Paula and I the real improvement was that we now had a proper bathroom without a hideous water tank suspended over the bath! The station also possessed two gardens at the rear allocated to the flats and also a grassed area around the station itself.

The only drawback to my new posting appeared to be the fact that the sergeant in charge, Sgt 379 Fred Parks, had a bit of a reputation for being a 'Martinet', a stickler for detail and discipline, and one to watch. It was he who was living in Flat 1. This might be difficult!

However, I had a cunning plan.

7

Ilminster Section

Before I was able to put my cunning plan into action, I was advised that I had to go on yet another course. This one was as a direct result of my posting to Ilminster.

Ilminster was a rural section, and in the early 70s such stations were only issued with one car, the sergeant's car. It was therefore an absolute requirement that all constables posted to the section should hold a full motorcycle licence and be proficient enough to be authorised to ride a fully equipped police motorcycle. In my case, the problem was that I had never ridden a motorcycle in my life.

And so it transpired that one very cold Monday morning in February 1970 I found myself reporting to the now abandoned wartime airfield in Culmstock in the hills above Taunton, for the first day of my two-week police motorcycle course. There were eight of us on the course, two others like me were total beginners. We were split into two groups of four, each group with an instructor in charge. We were introduced to our motorcycle for that first week of the course, a 250cc BSA Bantam.

I spent the first two hours learning the intricacies of a 250cc air-cooled engine, how to start it and how to change gear, etc. Then riding up and down the old runway and then the perimeter track. The afternoon saw us riding on open roads, around Culmstock and being urged to go faster and faster by our instructors.

The next day we rode to Bristol on the A38, and then back again via the A37, A303 and local roads to Culmstock. I was a bit saddle sore and cold when we got back. The next day we went to Barnstable in Devon and Thursday to Exmouth. The final day was test day and we swapped instructors. Both instructors were qualified and licensed testers. It clearly would not have been correct for the instructor to test his own students hence the reason for them swapping. The day was spent in and around Taunton in heavy traffic, each student in turn being followed closely by the tester who was watching us closely. We all passed! It might seem unusual for complete novices to receive their full motorcycle licences in only five days, but remember we were under close instruction by experts for almost eight hours a day and had covered hundreds of miles. But that was only the end of week one.

At the start of week two we were instructed to report to Taunton Division HQ garages where a number of 500cc Triumph Tiger Twin motorcycles had been allocated for our use. This machine was a quite formidable proposition for someone like me, who until one week ago had never even sat on a motorcycle let alone ridden one. The 250cc BSA

Bantam had been relatively easy to learn on, but this beast was going to be more of a challenge! In the first instance it was quite heavy when stationary, so you had to ensure that its weight was kept in balance and upright. If you weren't careful when pulling it onto its main stand it was easy to lose balance and then it would be very hard to stop it from falling over. We spent some time learning its basic daily maintenance, before starting up and venturing out onto the road. The rest of the day was spent in and around Taunton Division getting used to our new charge.

Each day then saw greater distances and higher average speeds being achieved although it must be remembered that this was intended as a basic motorcycle course and we were not being taught to be road traffic officers. The force was proud of its driving school standards and this course was part of it.

Our instructors would concentrate on each of us in turn, powering on ahead and patting his rear offside pannier indicating that that should be where we were to position ourselves. He knew our capabilities and was testing and developing them all the time. On the final Thursday we went up the A4 to Heathrow and back, each of us being extended for a considerable distance with the others trying to keep up. It was an enjoyable penultimate day.

Finally on Friday the two instructors swapped over again and re-tested each others' students. This test was not for a full licence, because we had achieved that at the end of week one. This test was for a 'County Authorisation'. We all passed and it meant that henceforth we were authorised to ride police motorcycles of up to 500cc on general police duties. We were not authorised to undertake road motor patrol duties (traffic officers' duties) which required a more advanced course.

Now I could undertake the full range of duties required of me as a constable on Sgt 378 Parks' Ilminster section. It had an establishment of nine constables. Four constables, of which I was one, were responsible for mainly foot patrol duties in and around Ilminster.

Four other constables lived in residential beat stations in South Petherton, Buckland St Mary, Seavington St Michael and Ilton.

The ninth constable was the residential beat officer for Ilminster itself, PC Alan Fitchet, who due to his long service and experience, lived in his own house on an estate in Ilminster.

All four residential beat officers generally worked 8 am–4 pm shifts, or 4 pm– 12 midnight, although on Fridays and Saturdays the late shifts tended to become 6 pm to 2 am to cover for occasional weekend disorder problems. Each of the RBOs was allocated a 500 CC motorcycle although these were gradually replaced by Ford Escort vans.

Between us, the four Ilminster town constables covered the standard 6–2, 2–10, and 10–6 am shifts that I had worked at Taunton. Except that here we were on our own. When we left the station, we locked it up behind us and patrolled alone. We had no radio; Taunton the nearest manned station, was over 15 miles away, far beyond the range of personal radios in police use in those days. So instead we made points at telephone kiosks instead. That meant that from 25 minutes past the hour until 35 minutes past the hour – 10 minutes – we stood outside pre-arranged telephone kiosks in case the control room at Taunton wanted to tell us something. Once we left that position we were lost to them again for a further 50 minutes!

Today that will sound almost Victorian, and in some respects policing in the smaller and rural townships of Somerset had not changed much since the early days. Without radio and thinly spread, we were very much on our own. You quickly learned how to handle yourself and how to deal with all sorts of issues. If you were really in trouble you did have your whistle, but as there were usually no other officers to help you, you had to rely on members of the public to assist. Luckily, Ilminster by and large was very peaceable. However if you did have to arrest someone, you had to manhandle them up through the streets, up a steep hill to the police station, unlock the back door, and then get them into the single cell. Having done all that, now your problems really started, because you had to get the sergeant out of bed to accept your prisoner! Not calculated to make you that popular.

That was where my cunning plan was centred! I had to gain the confidence of Fred Parks. I was still on probation at that stage, with at least eight months still to go until the important two-year confirmation point. So I could not allow my inexperience to shade his opinion of me.

I had spotted as soon as we moved in, that there was a huge difference in Fred's garden and mine – they were both the same size and shape, only separated by a close boarded fence. However, Fred's garden was immaculate, whilst mine was in a very poor state indeed. I was clearly going to have to develop a very keen love of gardening. So on my very first day off, I was out there digging my heart out. I really didn't know very much about it, but I had often seen my dad digging in his garden, so it was obviously the thing to do. Very soon Fred was looking over the top of the garden fence looking very much like the cartoon character 'Chad'. "Very good, Allinson," he said. "It's nice to see someone taking an interest in his garden, keen gardener are you?" "Oh yes," I replied, "I love it." "Excellent," he said. "Would you like some raspberry canes?" "Oh no thanks," I replied. "I don't have any raspberries!" This appeared to give Fred some indigestion and he went in. Not a good start!

Nevertheless, I soon settled into the new routine. Despite Fred's off-putting reputation he was actually a very good boss. A good sergeant! He ensured that the station was well run and that we all did our very best to ensure that we provided the very best service to the residents and businesses that made up the small town of Ilminster.

Our regular daytime foot patrols of the centre of the town ensured that traffic could flow properly through the area and also that through our day-to-day contact with the small town centre retailers, our knowledge of what was going on locally was constantly updated.

One of my priority duties during Fridays and Saturdays during the summer months was traffic control on the two main pedestrian crossings of the A303 through the town. This major trunk route would rapidly grind to a halt if you didn't regulate those pedestrian crossings. Traffic tailbacks would build up very quickly over many miles causing hours of delays.

Ilminster section was twinned with Chard section a few miles to the south. Chard was the larger of the two towns and like Ilminster straddled a major route to the southwest of England. Ilminster was on the A303 and Chard the A30.

Chard section was organised in exactly the same way as Ilminster, with four constables covering Chard town, and a similar number of RBOs lived in detached station houses in the surrounding countryside.

Chard town constables worked the same shifts as their Ilminster colleagues, and when on nights worked together after 2 am as a mobile night crime car. The two section sergeants took it in turns to be the sergeant on call for the week, The beat constable on night shift in each town patrolled on foot in his town until 1 am, taking his refreshments in his own station before the two joined together at 2 am using the car belonging to whichever sergeant was NOT on call. Our task was to check all vulnerable property, building sites and explosive stores, etc., on the two sections until we went off duty at 6 am.

In my case, I was twinned with my colleague PC 1000 Russell Kent. We knew each other very well as Russell was one month senior to me when we were both under training at Chantmarle. Russell obviously fancied himself as an expert rabbit catcher, and I recall one night when we were on a joint anti-crime patrol, we happened on a large open area that was in the process of being developed. There were a huge number of rabbits there and Russell decided he was going to get one of them. I stopped the car and he got out pulling his truncheon out of his pocket as he did so. I saw him start to wind up the truncheon in circles over his head, faster and faster whilst gripping the leather thong in his hand. Suddenly he threw it at one of the groups of rabbits. Unfortunately, the leather thong must have caught on one of his fingers because instead of hurtling towards the rabbits the truncheon shot downwards at an angle and bounced off the bonnet of my sergeant's car, leaving a big dent before disappearing into some undergrowth nearby! The rabbits scattered immediately and I'm sure I heard them laughing!

Now we had two problems. First we had to find Russell's truncheon, and that took some time, but there was also the problem of the dent in Sgt Park's bonnet.

Luckily that problem was resolved a little later, for whilst checking another building site, It appeared that the vibration caused by the movement of our car must have unsteadied a pile of bricks and one of them toppled onto the bonnet of the car. It was just one of those things I suppose. But I never allowed Russell to chase rabbits again.

We soon had an example of how the best intentions can go wrong. Sgt Parks had a visit from one of the Taunton inspectors one day. This relatively new and very keen inspector had decided to inspect minutely all of the station's books and records. Fred, being a stickler for detail of course, passed this close inspection of his records with no difficulty at all, until it came to the inspection of the found property cupboard. This tightly packed cupboard contained all of the found goods that the public had found and had then brought into the police station. Standing orders instructed that members of the public bringing in such property should be given the choice of leaving the property with us, or keeping it themselves after leaving us with their names and addresses, etc. Then if the loser called us, they would be directed to the finder's house to collect their property. This second option rarely happened, and the majority of found property always ended up in the sergeant's cupboard. Regulations required the sergeant to perform a monthly check of the cupboard in order to confirm that all of the property was accounted for.

This time the officiously keen inspector had criticised our sergeant for allowing too much property to accumulate!

Sgt Parks in turn subsequently berated us for not persuading more finders of property to agree to look after the property that they had found!

A few days later on a Saturday morning I was on early turn and had relieved PC 734 John Crosby who had been on the night shift. During our handover, John had told me that he had had a funny occurrence during his refreshment break when at about 1.15 am a passing lorry driver had brought in a large white rabbit, which he had discovered hopping down the middle of the A303! John said that in accordance with the sergeant's instructions he had persuaded the lorry driver to keep the rabbit.

I thought no more about it, and completed my early turn property checks in the town, returning to the station at about 9 am to cook my breakfast. At around 9.30 am the station front door bell had rung and on answering it I found a young mother outside, accompanied by her young son who was visibly upset.

I asked her what the problem was, to which she replied, "He's lost his white rabbit!" I smiled broadly, inviting her into the enquiry office, and I went around to the other side of the counter, reaching for the very impressive found property book. "Your white rabbit, young man, is in Penzance," I almost shrieked in my disbelief. The young mum then also burst into tears, and as a result I spent the next two hours tracing the trucking company the driver worked for, finally persuading them to deliver the white rabbit back to Ilminster the next time that they were passing. Fred soon heard about the incident, and rapidly changed his instructions.

I had now been at Ilminster for over six months and was still on probation, attending probationary training once a month. Many of the probationers that attended the same monthly training sessions found the whole process irksome, and as a result only did what was required. But in contrast, I found the study sessions helpful, realising that if I wanted to go further I would need to pass the sergeants exam as soon as possible. The passing of the sergeants examination and also the later inspectors exam (if applicable), were required prior to promotion in all UK police forces. However, the exams were merely academic qualifications and did not in themselves guarantee promotion. They did however allow you to perform temporary duty in the higher rank when there was a vacancy caused by sickness or leave, etc.

In that way you were able to demonstrate your readiness for a substantive promotion.

My point of two years' service arrived in October 1970 and I was formally confirmed as a constable in the Somerset and Bath Constabulary later that month. Not much changed of course and my duties at Ilminster continued as before.

As Christmas approached that year I was made aware of a tradition that existed in Ilminster that I had never experienced before. On Christmas eve, the police officers serving in the town all took their turkeys ready prepared in baking trays down to the local bakers shop where he placed them in his bread ovens on Christmas morning. We collected them later Christmas morning, ready for our Christmas lunch at home. Wonderful.

In the spring of 1971, I sat my sergeants qualifying examination at the force training centre Cannonsgrove. Thanks to the excellent training regime during my probationary period I did not find it at all difficult. There were three separate papers – law, general police duties and road traffic procedures – all of which required a high pass mark. Nevertheless, I was stunned three months later to learn not just that I had passed, but that I had secured a level of pass mark that placed me in the top 200 in the country!

To be in the top 200 position nationally gave me an automatic regional interview for appointment to the next 'Special Course' at the Police Staff College at Bramshill. Selection for the year-long Special Course would have resulted in an immediate promotion to the rank of sergeant, and further promotion to the rank of inspector after 12 months of operational service as a sergeant. However I was not ultimately successful. I did manage to pass the regional element, but sadly did not succeed in the final three-day extended interviews at Churchill College Cambridge. Most successful candidates were university educated.

Nevertheless it was obvious that the chief was very happy with my progress and I soon commenced an extended period of acting sergeant duties both at Ilminster and Chard, and occasionally too back in Taunton. In addition I was awarded a three-month 'Aid to CID' attachment at Taunton and also a three-month attachment to the Road Traffic Division. I was aware of it at the time, but several years later I discovered that despite failing the Staff College extended interviews, the chief had placed me on the force's own high potential scheme. I just thought that I was lucky getting those attachments!

By the summer of 1971 we realised that Paula was expecting a baby and our happiness was almost complete. We loved our life in Ilminster and everything was turning out well for us.

Police regulations in the early 70s permitted constables who had already passed the sergeants exam to sit the inspectors qualifying examination, even though they had not yet been promoted to sergeant. And so having continued with the required study, I took and subsequently passed the inspectors examination in late 1971.

By late February 1972, Paula's condition was causing some concern in respect of raised blood pressure, and the condition known as pre-eclampsia. A period of complete bed rest was prescribed and she was admitted to the maternity unit at Yeovil General Hospital.

By 13th March, it seemed that the baby might soon be making an entrance. I was scheduled to work the 10 pm to 6 am shift that night, but arranged to finish earlier than usual and drove immediately to the hospital, arriving at 6 am on the 14th. The hospital staff confirmed that labour had indeed started, but nothing was going to happen very quickly and suggested that I should go home, and come back at about midday to see how things were progressing. I did as I was told. I returned as instructed at 12 midday, only to find that I was the proud father of a little girl, born at about 8.30 am! I was really upset at missing the birth of my daughter, but the excitement of seeing her in her cot made up for it. Paula stayed in hospital with Julie for ten days, before I was able to take my new family home to Ilminster. We were so happy to have Julie with us, and I guess that one of my abiding memories will always be of Paula standing in front of one of the windows in our flat overlooking the town and whispering to Julie, "Night night big world, see you in the morning!"

One evening in late 1972, whilst once again 'acting' at Ilminster, I was called to an incident which tested just about all of the skills that I had accumulated in recent months. It was a really foul night, very high winds were bringing down a number of trees and the rain was lashing down. Then at about 10 pm I received a call to a house in woodlands near the border between Chard and Ilminster. The call suggested that a shooting had occurred there. It was a house that I knew well as it was the home of a very disturbed young man, who I had had dealings with before. I was met at the door by a woman who was hysterical. I entered and immediately saw the body of the young lad lying on the floor. He was clearly dead, there could be no doubt of that. In the corner of the room sitting in a chair was his father holding what I knew to be a 4/10 shotgun. I secured the scene, moving both adults to another room after advising the father that he was under arrest on suspicion of causing the death of the deceased youth. I then used the radio in the sergeant's car to summon senior officers, the CID and scenes of crime officers. They very soon started to arrive and took over from me. Then I heard that the chief constable was on his way.

It might seem unusual, judged by today's standards, but in the early 1970s chief constables did still quite often attend significant incidents like this one. However I realised that due to the dreadful storm that was still raging, the chief, coming from the direction he was, would not be able to get past some fallen trees. So I arranged for a car to meet him, and to bring him to the scene via a different route. He stayed for about 20 minutes, seemed happy that all was being properly managed and left. I remained at the cottage for some time to ensure that everything was secured, and then made my way to Taunton Divisional HQ for reports and statements, etc. It was dawn before I got home to Ilminster Police Station.

Two days later I received a personal note from the chief constable, Kenneth Steele, (or KWL as we all called him), congratulating me on my handling of the incident. I was very relieved.

In January 1973 I received an invitation from the divisional detective chief inspector, to accompany him whilst he gave a drugs talk to a group in Wellington. I asked Sgt Parks for permission and was somewhat surprised when he readily agreed. My shift was changed to 6 pm to 2 am to accommodate it and Fred advised that I should do a foot patrol of the town centre on my return. In the event, however, I never did that foot patrol because the DCI insisted on us going for a drink after the talk, and he got me well and truly plastered. As a result, I went straight to bed as soon as I got home.

At 8.30 am the phone rang beside my bed and I immediately recognised the voice of the HQ administrative chief inspector, ordering me to attend the HQ in Taunton at 10.30 am in my best uniform. It appeared to me that somehow they had found out about my state of intoxication the night before and that I was on the carpet and facing the high jump!

I arrived at HQ 15 minutes early and was made to wait nervously in a small office until 10.30. Then without warning, I was marched in to see the chief constable, Kenneth Steele. He informed me that he was promoting me to the rank of sergeant, and that he was transferring me to Weston-super-Mare division, with effect from the 1st March 1973.

Paula and I were to be allocated a police house at 30 Manor Road, Weston-super-Mare. He shook my hand, told me to sit down and spoke to me for 20 minutes about leadership and what he expected of me. Then, still in a daze, I was ushered out!

It didn't dawn on me immediately, for I had not been expecting it to come quite in the way that it did, but I eventually realised that my promotion was one of the fastest involving someone who had not been part of the Special Course system. I felt extremely humbled, for I realised that many of my colleagues were at least as competent if not more so than me, but had not had the lucky turn of fate that I had experienced.

Weston Super Mare Police Station

8

Patrol Sergeant
Weston-super-Mare

Looking back on it now, the next few months at Weston-super-Mare were probably some of the most difficult of my entire police career. This was entirely due to my somewhat rapid promotion and my relative inexperience. I had completed 18 months at Taunton, and then about two years at Ilminster, which of course was relatively quiet. With less than four years' total service it was clearly essential for me to learn how to be a supervisor very quickly.

In contrast to Ilminster, Weston-super-Mare Division, being very close geographically to the city of Bristol, was probably the busiest division in the Somerset And Bath Force area. In addition, the 1970s had become the years of the Mods and Rockers disturbances, and Weston-super-Mare like many other seaside resorts, certainly had its fair share of the disturbances.

At Ilminster, I had been used to patrolling alone, but now I was in charge of my own section of eight men and was responsible for their welfare, proper development and for their operational deployment. The section, or group as it was now being called, comprised of two or three longer service constables but the remaining five were all probationers of varying lengths of service.

The divisional senior officers had anticipated that I would need a period of acclimatisation and so had arranged for me to spend a full week of night shifts working with a very experienced and older sergeant, Sgt 479 Sam Seaman.

And so feeling very self conscious in my new uniform with its dazzling woven silver sergeant's stripes, I paraded for duty with Sam's section as he briefed them for their duties. He read out all the recent crime reports, missing people, local stolen cars, etc., and then gave each man his area of patrol and refreshment time. The patrol area allocation sounded a bit like this, "223 Town Centre North, 994 Town Centre South, 78, seafront, 118 Anti Violence unit, with 998, 326 Oldmixon area, Bill – Front Office, Harry – Control Room."

The briefing carried on in similar fashion each night with some variation so that the officers did not get stale. However, on the last two nights of the week I noticed that the constable who had previously been known as 78, had now become Tony! This seemed very strange to me and so on our last night together I decided to ask Sam why PC 78 had suddenly become Tony? He looked at me as if I was daft and said, "It's bloody simple innit?" My reply was, "No, not to me it's not." He grinned and said, "Well thems with numbers, they're not real policemen, they're just probationers, but young Tony he got his two years in on Friday, so he's a real policeman now, sos I can call him Tony."

Life was simpler then!

Weston-super-Mare took a lot of getting used to after South Somerset. One thing that Paula and I never accepted was that the sea was brown, not blue as we had known on the Dorset Coast. From a policing viewpoint too it was very different. Summer weekends were very busy indeed. Seafront and esplanade patrols were a vital element in our planning.

Policewomen had not yet been integrated into fully operational section or group staffing, but instead were organised into what was known as the Police Women's department. They were supervised by their own female sergeant, and specialised in dealing with women and children who for one reason or other had come to police attention. However, when not primarily engaged in their specialist duties, they could be loaned to the operational section sergeant on early or lates, and would patrol in company with male constables. Generally speaking, they did not work full night shifts, but did quite often work 4–midnight or 6 pm–2 am shifts. They were great to have with us, and their presence often calmed down domestic disputes and even pub brawls.

One aspect of Weston-super-Mare that did take a bit of getting used to was the annoying habits of the seagulls! You could do a foot patrol of the seafront and town area just before dawn and everything would be fine, but then only half an hour later when it got light, the seagulls would have emptied the contents of all the rubbish bins all over the roads, in an effort to find food left by late night revellers!

By the late summer of 1973, all of the sections at Weston-super-Mare were carrying a significant number of vacancies. However, the summer rush was still on, and at the busy weekends our ability to deal with disorder in the town was often stretched to the limit.

Because of our depleted numbers I resorted to the use of bluff tactics in order to boost our apparent numbers, telling my guys to drive around in one car for 30 minutes or so, and then come back to the station and take out a different one for a while, and to keep swapping them around. This bluff tactic was very effective with the anti-violence team. We would put out six officers in the anti-violence long-wheel base Land Rover, then bring them back in and send them out in three double-crewed cars etc.

It was, of course, all bluff, but it did seem to work. It certainly gave the troublemakers the impression that there were loads of us about.

By the end of that first summer I had grown used to policing Weston-super-Mare, and was enjoying being part of the station's establishment. One oddity that the division was noted for was the number of officers bearing animal names in their surnames. We had PCs Doe, Fox, Badger and Beaver. Sergeants Pigeon, Rabbits and Bullock.

I noticed with great satisfaction that due to the exposure to the sea, salt, sun and rain my overly bright silver stripes had now tarnished to a much more experienced dull rust colour. I was no longer the new and inexperienced sergeant!

Like every seaside town, Weston also had a high proportion of retired and elderly residents. They, as you would expect, brought with them a requirement for sympathetic attention.

In particular, the station was constantly visited by an elderly lady who had a very unusual problem! She explained that her house had been built a few years ago directly over the hotline which ran between No 10 Downing Street in London and the White House in Washington, USA. And whenever the prime minister was talking on the phone to the president of the USA, it set off dreadful vibrations in her house, and what were we going to do about it? At first the front office staff were very sympathetic and polite, but after a while they were clearly starting to find the need to be sympathetic a bit wearing. The problem was brought to me the next time that she came in, and I took her into my office and listened to her story. She was a lovely old lady but clearly had a bit of a fixation on this perceived problem, and so I promised to look into it for her. She left obviously in a happier frame of mind.

I had remembered that 223 Doe was a dedicated 'roll your own' smoker and that in his locker he had loads of empty tobacco tins, some of which he had scraped the paint and advertising off, and as a result they were very shiny. I persuaded him to let me have one and in it I placed a large red battery out of one of our radio transmitters and a smaller yellow one out of one of the receivers. A few coloured wires completed the job.

Two days later I called in on the lady and explained that I had a friend in the Home Office in London who understood her problem, and that he had given me this machine which I had to bury in her back garden and it would stop all of the vibrations. She was delighted and so with great ceremony I produced a spade which I had brought with me and dug a foot deep hole in her garden. The tin was buried and the soil returned as before. And it worked!

She didn't come in again for over a year, and even then just to ask for the batteries to be changed.

That October another incident occurred which almost had the potential to get me into trouble. I had been sitting in the control room one afternoon when a 999 call came in from a Mrs Fish living in Sand Bay, to the effect that there were bones sticking up out of the sand in Sand Bay. I looked at the message and wrongly assumed that I was subject of a wind up by one of the officers – Mrs Fish, complaining of bones on the beach? Oh yes, a likely story, and so I screwed up the message. Some time later I answered a second call from the good lady, now obviously rather cross that no one had been to see her!

Conscious that this could cause a complaint, I went to see her myself and she took me around a small headland to where there were indeed three large curved bones sticking out of the sand. I set about clearing some of the sand and within a fairly short time had revealed two skeletons! Clearly this was serious and once again I was calling for the CID and senior staff. My inspector arrived to check all was in order and then pointed to the middle finger of my left hand that was bleeding. I commented that I had cut it on the eye socket of one of the skulls and he became very concerned insisting that I went immediately to Weston General Hospital, which at that time was in the centre of the town. I did as I was told and was seen by a casualty nurse who enquired when I last had a tetanus jab. I jokingly replied, "Probably four years ago at least" and she said, "I'll just give you a booster!" I started to roll up my sleeve and she grinned saying, "Oh no, trousers down, bend over!"

I'm sure that that syringe was as big as a double-barrelled shotgun! I've never trusted nurses since!

The origin of those skeletons was never resolved. The bones were sent to Bristol University for carbon dating. The result that came back was not terribly helpful in that we were advised that they were probably not less than 50 years old, or more than 500 years old! That really didn't give us a lot to go on.

There was nothing to suggest the cause of death and the only remnants of clothing was what appeared to be the sole of a leather sandal.

The matter was referred to the coroner and it was finally decided that they were probably fishermen who died at sea centuries ago.

Weston-super-Mare was the location for my second arrest for murder. Very late one night, I received a report of a stabbing at a club just behind the seafront. Other units had also been dispatched but this was clearly one where a supervisor would be required. In the event, I recall that I was the first police unit to arrive, although there was an ambulance already in the car park. I saw a small crowd of people bending over a body lying in the car park, and immediately went over. There were ambulance staff treating the victim but from the amount of blood on the floor this was very serious indeed.

A trail of blood lead into the club premises and I followed it into the main club area where a lot of people were standing around talking quietly, many appeared to be in shock. I asked who knew what had happened and who was responsible for the attack on the young man I had seen in the car park. No one really said much but several pointed up a circular iron stairway that gave access to the floor above the club premises. It was clearly down to me to go up! I climbed the staircase and found myself on a darkened landing looking down a dark corridor, to where I could see a light coming from what looked like an office. I walked down the corridor and looked through the open door. Sitting in a chair beside a desk was a man dressed in dark leathers, he was in his late 20s/early 30s. I told him that I had found a man lying in the car park outside who was clearly very seriously injured, and that I had followed a trail of blood into this club. Did he know anything about it?

He leant forward and pulled quite a large knife out of the top of one of his motorcycle boots. At this point my mouth went dry and I was wondering what best to do, when he put the knife onto the top of the desk and said, "Down the station I suppose!" I initially arrested him for committing grievous bodily harm, but as soon as I got him downstairs I was advised that the man in the car park was deceased. So the arrest was for one of murder. I was tied up dealing with the aftermath of that one for several days.

By now, Paula and I were really enjoying Weston-super-Mare. Our house in Manor Road was great, although it had suffered from a very long period of low expenditure once it had become a police house. Probably built immediately after the Second World War, the semi-detached house had been purchased by the police authority as the divisional superintendent's house. Accordingly, it was in a very nice area and stood alone as a police house amongst many privately owned properties.

But now it had been downgraded to a sergeant's house and expenditure had dried up. In contrast, our attached next door neighbours had maintained their own house to a very high standard. The comparison between the two houses was therefore quite stark. But even though there was that problem, we did love our time at 33 Manor Road.

By mid 1974, despite now being very happy at Weston-super Mare, we were both becoming increasingly concerned by the age and vulnerability of both of our mothers now living in council flats in differing parts of Yeovil. So at my next annual staff review I put in a welfare request for any vacancy for a sergeant's position on Yeovil Division.

As it happened, there soon was a vacancy for a station sergeant at the Yeovil Divisional HQ at Petters Way Yeovil, and I was offered the position and accepted. We were allocated a police house in Westland Road, Yeovil, making the move in September of that year. By now Paula was expecting our second child.

From a social and family welfare viewpoint the move to Yeovil was excellent. It allowed us to ensure that both our mothers were well looked after in their later years, and also allowed us to rekindle old friendships that we had not been able to easily maintain for a number of years.

However, from my point of view the role of station sergeant at Yeovil Police HQ was not very demanding.

The shift patterns were a much easier 8–4 and 4–12 pattern, with the very occasional full night shift thrown in to cover a patrol sergeant off due to sickness. However, Yeovil was very quiet after Weston, and if the truth be known I was not getting the challenges that I needed to maintain my interest. I felt that I was coasting.

Our son Jeremy was born in Yeovil Maternity Hospital in April 1975 and this time I was there. I was not going to be cheated a second time! It was a fantastic experience and I really needed that cup of tea after it was all done!

We took Jeremy home to Westland Road a few days later – the family was growing.

But just then a new opportunity presented itself, and it was one that I went after with great enthusiasm. It had come to my notice that Sergeant Eric January was about to retire as the detached rural sergeant at Wincanton.

The post of rural section sergeant in the force in those days was a very important one. Each rural sergeant was in sole charge of a geographically large section, with a staff of usually about ten officers and a civilian clerk. Occasionally, the section also included a traffic warden.

In the case of Wincanton section, the area covered included the two small towns of Bruton and Castle Cary, plus several villages too. The twin A303 and A30 trunk roads both passed through the section in similar fashion as they had at Ilminster. Geographically, the section covered all of the territory from the Wiltshire and Dorset boundaries in the east, almost to Yeovil in the southwest. The western boundary was the main A37 road to Bristol.

The area covered by the section also included the strategically important Royal Naval Air Station at Yeovilton near Ilchester. The base was the main training establishment for Fleet Air Arm fixed-wing pilots!

I applied for the forthcoming vacancy and was delighted to learn very quickly that my application had been successful. Wincanton section was mine!

I was not to know it then, but the next four years were to become probably the most satisfying of my entire career.

Wincanton Police Station

9

Rural Sergeant

Wincanton Section

We had been allocated the sergeant's house at No 7 Locks Lane, Wincanton, just about 30 yards away from the station. The whole complex was only a matter of a few years old and the four police houses were of quite modern design, certainly nothing like any of the others that I had seen previously. We considered ourselves to be very lucky.

The police station was also quite new. It featured a front enquiry desk and a general office for the civilian clerk. Behind that was the sergeant's office and then up a few stairs to a slightly raised level was a large parade room with a conference and briefing area. At a lower level was the rear station yard with garages for two cars and a van. There was plenty of room.

On my first day at the station, Sergeant January who had already effectively retired, had come in civilian clothes to hand over to me and to go through the station books in some detail. He introduced me to PC 349 Ron Stingemore, the senior man on the section, who was also soon to retire. PCs 249 Bonham, PC 1139 Tony Clifford, PC 1175 Trevor Thomas and PC 1209 Alex McCartney made up the four-man response team.

The small towns and villages in the very large section were covered by a team of residential beat officers, each living in a police house with a dedicated police office attached. PC 602 Gerry Hawkins looked after Bruton, PC 257 Gwyne Phillips looked after Castle Cary, PC 675 Dave Cranmer looked after Bayford, PC 172 Mike Stanton, was at Templecombe, PC 321 Malcolm Baker at Marston Magna, and PC1091 Rod Allen at Milborne Port. In all, ten constables and one traffic warden were allocated to Wincanton Section. They were supplemented by an extensive group of special constables – mainly local farmers who tended to work with their detached beat officers on a regular basis.

One of my first tasks was to meet the local magistrates, because one of my responsibilities as the town sergeant was to prosecute cases before the Magistrates Court each Monday morning. I recall that the chair at the time was Mrs Montgomery. Captain Cunningham RN was I believe the Deputy. Others were Mrs Hobhouse, and local undertaker Mr Harold Miles. The magistrates clerk was Peter Clarke.

I also had the pleasure of meeting the coroner for southeast Somerset. He was a highly regarded local solicitor Mr John Fenton-Rutter. I formed the opinion that he was an outstanding man, blessed with a skilled and enquiring mind. He was one that I always enjoyed serving during the many coroner's inquests that I attended during my time at Wincanton.

Paula and I settled into life in Wincanton very quickly. It helped that I still remembered the area quite well. I had not previously worked with any of my officers before, but they were all clearly dedicated to providing a good service, not only to the residents of Wincanton, but also to the other communities spread over the vast section. The crime rate was remarkably low and the detection rate commendably high. I was conscious that I should be very careful to maintain that standard.

The sergeant's car was a Hillman Avenger, and a second Avenger was also available for use by the four Wincanton officers covering the full 24-hour shift pattern. Unlike my Ilminster days when the detached residential beat officers each had a motorbike, my six RBOs spread across a much wider section now each had a Ford Escort van.

I found that my days were often quite busy keeping on top of a considerable amount of administration. On this section there were more firearm and shotgun renewals than had been the case at Ilminster, and each one had to be allocated to the most appropriate officer for action. It was pleasing to note that all ten officers were active in enforcing the law, and as a result a number of prosecution files had to be examined and decisions taken as to prosecution or caution.

As the officer in charge at Wincanton, I was also responsible for prosecuting all cases coming before Wincanton Magistrates Court, except of course where a defendant was represented by a solicitor, that being the case a suitable legally qualified solicitor acted for us.

My direct supervisory officers were Chief Inspector Fred Sandy and Inspector Jim Bowler, both based in an office at Yeovil divisional HQ. They were responsible for all the detached sections in the division including Wincanton, Somerton and Crewkerne sections. Both took a low operational profile, concentrating on administrational matters, leaving their experienced section sergeants to get on with their job.

There was one additional duty that was the responsibility of the Wincanton section sergeant. That was of course Wincanton races! The very racecourse that years before I had walked past twice a day on my journey to and from school in Wincanton, now fell under my responsibility to police on race days.

Fred Sandy explained that there was one small but important perk that came with my role as the section sergeant at Wincanton. I must always ensure that one of my allocated rest days would fall on each scheduled race day. The Wincanton sergeant was always required to attend the racecourse on race days, and so as a result would claim overtime payment for working a rest day!

He explained that my role as a detached section sergeant meant that I now carried a full 24-hour responsibility for the section, seven days a week throughout the year. I would receive no extra payment for the additional responsibility, and so the ability to claim overtime at the races was classed as compensation for the unpaid heavier responsibility. The new role also required that on at least two weekends per month, I was required to work 9 am to 1 pm and 9 pm to 1 am split shifts. This was outside police regulations and a downside of having the extra responsibility of being a rural detached section Sergeant!

Soon after we arrived at Wincanton I was delighted to receive a very kind invitation from Major and Mrs Davie to join them for dinner at Charlton Musgrove House. We were very happy to accept. Even today nearly 40 years later, I still find it strange to describe my feelings when entering that great house again, but for the first time through the front door!

Obviously both the Major and Mrs Davie were much older than I remembered, but they were still lovely people, and they seemed to be delighted that I had been appointed the town sergeant in Wincanton.

From the day I joined the police service, our social life had become quite limited. The initial period away at the training centre, and the subsequent posting to Taunton had dramatically reduced the amount of contact that both of us had with our old friends. Since then, any social life had tended to be with fellow officers and their families. I knew that Paula especially was feeling quite cut off.

Then quite suddenly, and within a few months of our arrival in Wincanton, I received an invitation from one of the two veterinary surgeons in the town, to accompany him to a meeting of the local Round Table.

This group of local farmers and professional men met on the 1st and 3rd Tuesday of every month to enjoy a meal together, to plan charity fundraising events and also social events such as dances, skittles matches and any other event that they believed might assist in their charitable enterprises. I found them to be great company and very importantly were unlikely to cause me any embarrassment in my position as the town police sergeant.

Crucially too, their wives became members of a group known as the 'Ladies Circle'. They too met regularly for meals and to arrange their own social events and fundraising. Paula joined them quite soon and immediately formed some firm friendships.

Quite soon after I arrived, work commenced on the important Wincanton by-pass. The A303 had long since become the main trunk route from London to the far southwest, and the parallel A30 had been downgraded. However, the result of that was a dreadful bottleneck at Wincanton as heavy goods traffic and ordinary motorists crawled through the town. Work on the by-pass was going to take a couple of years, but it would all be worth it in the end!

However once the work commenced we experienced a problem that I don't think anyone had expected. The route of the new by-pass looped around to the south of the town but there were two or three places where it had to cross the A303 itself. The actual crossing places had been well designed but inevitably where the huge earth movers crossed the main road, they did leave a lot of mud on the road surface. The contractors had anticipated the problem and were going to great lengths to wash the surface down. But however hard they tried, a fine layer of slippery mud and clay remained.

Suddenly we were finding that HGVs heading east through the town, climbing the steep incline towards the town centre, were losing traction and were often unable to get up the hill. The problem mainly occurred on damp days. Dry days were not a problem, neither were wet days, but on damp days chaos quickly reigned.

The solution required the local authority and the contractor to work closely together, to reduce the problem by gritting the road surface.

We had a low crime rate in Wincanton but just occasionally things went awry. Despite having the giant Cow and Gate Milk factory in the town, there was actually only one milk supplier to the residents, and over the years in order to ensure that they didn't suffer from people not paying their bills on time, the dairy had developed a system whereby people had to put out a tin each night containing the correct money for however many bottles of milk were required that morning. Apparently, the system had existed for years and despite being a nuisance to some, it worked. Until suddenly people were not getting the number of bottles they had expected. The correct amount of money had allegedly not been put out. The problem started slowly, but gradually got worse, and very soon it was brought to our attention.

The dairy was losing money and the residents had dry cornflakes!

An investigation was mounted and several milkmen were spoken to, but it clearly wasn't down to them. I think it was Dave Cranmer that sorted it. He normally worked an 8-4 day shift but decided one day to book on early and to keep observations. He found that two paper boys had discovered a way of supplementing their income, by taking small amounts from each tin they found whilst posting the papers through letter boxes. Major crime outbreak solved!

But now I found myself in dispute with the divisional chief inspector over crime statistics. Whilst the crime had remained undetected he had insisted that it was one continuous offence. But now we had culprits, he was demanding that each individual theft was recorded and shown as detected!.

That would certainly improve his divisional crime figures, but as far as I was concerned it would show a huge rise in crime in Wincanton, and I was there to keep it down.

In the end, my spirited resistance won that battle, but I wasn't very popular with the DCI for a while!

The section, straddling as it did both of the main trunk routes to the southwest, was frequently required to deal with a number of very serious road accidents. Sadly, many of those accidents were fatal ones and in each case the coroner, John Fenton Rutter, would later phone me and ask me to arrange for a coroners inquest jury to be assembled on a particular date. The venue was always the local Magistrates Court in North Road.

I had realised soon after my arrival at Wincanton that such requests were to happen from time to time, and so set about compiling a list of local people who were willing to give up their time to attend inquests acting as the jury. It soon became evident that there were a number of local dairy farmers who were ideal for the task. Dairy farmers were by their very nature worldly wise and although very busy in the early mornings and late afternoons could often spare some time in the mid mornings and early afternoons. There were also several local business men that I knew would help.

Each inquest would normally follow the same agenda, witnesses were called, or statements would be read out, and the facts surrounding the incident recorded. Then John Fenton Rutter would sum up the facts to the jury and clarify the verdicts open to them, usually accidental death or on occasions death by misadventure. Once the verdict was reached, JFR would reach down under his desk and produce a brown calico bag tied up with a drawstring. He would thank the jury for their deliberations and then say, "Now, I've got your conduct money here, £1.25p, but you don't want it do you? You want me to give it to the sergeant, for the Police Benevolent Fund, don't you? Yes that's right." In the four years I was at Wincanton, I never saw anyone actually collect their conduct money. However the section's contribution to the divisional Police Benevolent Fund was always the best in the area!

There was one occasion however that I will never forget, and which firmly cemented in me the admiration that I held for the character of JFR.

He had called me in the usual way to arrange an inquest on a particular date and for me to obtain the services of a jury which I did. However, on the day of the inquest, the keys to the Magistrates Court, which were normally hanging on a hook in my office, had gone missing. I searched the station and put a call out to all my staff, but no one could throw any light as to where the missing keys might be.

Fearing a very serious complaint from JFR, I duly attended the court at the appointed time of 10 am, and waited in the rear car park with the witnesses and the jury. All attempts to get in had failed.

JFR drove into the car park in his large Mercedes and I went over to meet him. I explained about the missing keys and my failed attempts to gain access and he replied, "Oh dear, that's a bit embarrassing isn't it? Well, everyone's here now anyway. I'll tell you what, it's a nice day, so I will sit in my cars' driving seat, with my feet outside the car. You arrange everyone around in a big semi-circle, and we will hear the case out here!" And that is what we did. The facts were recorded, the jury came to their verdict and everyone went home quite satisfied. I never heard another thing about it from JFR, but I still shudder to think about the fuss that a lesser man might have made. Nothing ever fazed him.

The keys miraculously reappeared on the hook two days later.

Natural progression brought about a number of changes to staff during my period as the section sergeant. Ron Stingemore retired soon after I arrived, and PC 321 Malcom Baker left Marston Magna station for a new career in the force training department, PC 1209 Alex McCartney moved from Win-canton to Marston Magna to replace him. PC 1097 Doug Johnson arrived to replace Alex, and PC 1174 Terry Raper replaced Ron Stingemore.

1976 proved to be a year of significant firsts for me. When I had been stationed in Yeovil, I had joined the Westland Aircraft Sports and Social Club, and had taken up .22 rifle shooting as a sport. I had actually become quite good at it, and now had an average score in competition of 99.5/100. This was of course on a covered indoor range.

But when I moved to Wincanton, I had progressed to 'Full Bore' 7.62mm rifle shooting, on open military ranges, and was now shooting at county competition level. Somehow, the powers that be in the force had picked this up and now, together with another sergeant, Andy Gray, from Bristol, I was being sent as an experiment to the Royal Marines training centre at Lympstone in Devon to train as a sniper.

And so on one Sunday night in April 1976, I reported to CTCRM Lympstone to commence the Royal Marines Snipers Course. The force had equipped me with a 7.62MM snipers rifle fitted with telescopic sights. This was going to be interesting!

As a sergeant I was allocated a cabin in the sergeants' mess area and as I entered the cabin I noticed a note pinned to the door which said 'If you want tea or coffee in the morning put a tick in the box'. So I did.

At 6 am there was a loud knocking at the door and I said. "Come in!" The door crashed open and a voice said "Where's your mug?" I answered, "I haven't got a mug!" The voice replied loudly, "Sorry sir, no mug, no tea!" and the door slammed shut!

I then went over to the mess for breakfast. I sat at a vacant table and was approached by a steward obviously intent on taking my order. I said "A full breakfast please", meaning of course a full English breakfast. He looked at me a bit quizzically and went off. A few minutes later he returned with a large dinner plate literally covered in all manner of food. I was amazed at the amount of food on my plate and questioned what the reason was. His reply was, "Well if you want bacon and eggs you ask for bacon and eggs, if you want braised kidneys, you ask for braised kidneys, if you want sausages and bacon you ask for sausages and bacon! If you just say you want a breakfast you gets the lot." I was learning!

After my initial failure to obtain an early morning cup of tea, I soon acquired the necessary mug and so the next morning was confidently anticipating the tea orderly's arrival. There was the bang on the door, "Come in" I said. "Where's your mug?" the voice said.

"Over there," I replied and opened my eyes in time to see that the steward was carrying a large enamelled bucket full of tea into which he dipped my mug, filling it up. He placed it on a shelf and went out, slamming the door!

There were six marines on the course, four paratroopers and two police officers. Each of us was already classed as excellent marksmen, and it was evident that the course itself was more teaching the art of camouflage and concealment, the ability to stalk and approach a target unseen, and to shoot from difficult and unusual positions. The first few days were spent making our own Gillie suit. Essentially a paratrooper's smock re-enforced with a thick linoleum-type lining at the front and down the front of the trousers. This was because the sniper's main method of moving and crossing all terrains was by crawling on his belly! The Gillie suit and the rifle itself were also covered in hessian into which were fastened copious amounts of foliage.

Most days we would be taken either to Woodbury Common in south Devon or onto Dartmoor where we were assembled in a tight group. The senior instructor would point to a distant tree just visible on the horizon and tell us that at the bottom of that tree was an enemy observation post and we had to get within 100 metres of the observer and shoot him. We had of course been issued with blank 7.65mm ammunition! It was further explained that we would be given one minute from the word 'Go' to get out of sight, and then a maximum of three hours to get into a firing position and fire a blank round at the enemy observer. Just to make it even more difficult, each of us would be accompanied by an instructor walking within ten yards of our position so that the staff in the enemy observer's position would know where to look. If at any time we were spotted during that three hours we would fail that test. Even after we had got into position and successfully fired our rifle at the target observer, it was not the end of the test, for our walking instructor would then be told to move in to place his hand on our head. If the target could still not see us, we would be told to stand up, leaving our rifle in position, and the instructor would then lie down in our position in order to check that we had the telescopic sight correctly set for the prevailing wind and distance and that he could clearly see the target. Only if all that was correct could we claim a pass on that test.

The course lasted six weeks. It was very hard physical work and although we were fed very well indeed at the training centre, we all lost quite a bit of weight and were extremely fit at the end of it.

One strange thing always seemed to happen when we were on stalks or map reading exercises on Woodbury Common. We would be taken there in 3-ton military lorries and they would arrange to pick us up at the same spot at about 4 pm. But each day the transport would fail to arrive and we would be required to double march the three miles back to camp. It must have looked very strange to passers-by to see 12 trees jogging past carrying rifles!

I passed the course with the top 'sniper marksman' classification, but sadly when submitting my report to Force HQ at the conclusion of the six weeks I could not recommend that any further police officers be sent. Yes, it had slightly improved my shooting, especially at moving targets, but there was a critical difference in the requirement for an armed police officer. The military emphasis had been on camouflage and concealment, yet the armed police officer is required to give clear and final warnings etc. before using his weapon. The two tasks were very different. It was a smashing course though!

Soon after the sniper's course It was suggested that I should also undergo additional weapons training in order to become an authorised firearms officer or AFO. The course comprised of training in the use of various types of hand guns, both revolvers and semi-automatic pistols.

1976 was also the year of my first ever flight in an aeroplane. I had been having a pint in an Ilchester pub one weekend with a Mod Plod (military police) sergeant from RNAS Yeovilton. He had been waxing lyrical about all the different types of aircraft that he had flown in, and I had replied to the effect that I had never flown in an aircraft in my life. He immediately offered to arrange for me to have a flight, but in my experience it was the sort of thing that people often say, but hardly ever follow through with. Especially after a pint! So I was really impressed when halfway through Monday morning the phone rang and it was him calling to say he had arranged the flight and it was at 10 am on Thursday morning. The only complication he said was that I had to come in at 11 am on Wednesday for ejector seat training! My flight was going to be in a two-seat Hawker Hunter jet trainer. WHAT?!

The ejector seat training on Wednesday was no fun whatsoever. I had several hours of being measured and fitted with a flying suit and flying helmet, and then taken through practically every emergency thought possible and the dangers of the seat itself. How to remove and stow the safety pins and also how to refit them.

I was really very worried by the end of it all, and spent most of that night wondering how I could get out of it without losing face. There wasn't a way; I had told too many people!

The following morning I presented myself to the main gate at Yeovilton and was directed to the FRADU (Fleet Requirement and Direction Unit) office on the main flight line of the air station. There I was introduced to my pilot Brian Grant. He was friendly and exuded a huge air of competence and experience. So much so that as soon as he introduced himself, any nervousness that I might have been feeling, immediately melted away. He ensured that I was properly briefed. It was quite clear that this was no jolly flight, it was a proper operational sortie required by the Royal Navy that Brian was flying, and had I not been there he would have had to have flown it anyway.

The brief was that we would depart Yeovilton at 10.30, flying a south westerly route down over Devon and Cornwall, then passing overhead the Isles of Scilly and out into the western approaches of the North Atlantic. There we were to R/V with the Cruiser HMS Blake, who was now working back up to full efficiency after a major refit. Our task was to make initial radio contact with her and then to fly at certain altitudes and compass headings that she would request of us. Once we were able to confirm to her that we were exactly at the coordinates that she had given, her radio engineers would adjust and accurately calibrate their newly upgraded radar equipment.

We walked together out to the aircraft which Brian explained was a Hawker Hunter T Mk 8 naval training aircraft. The T Mk 8 was the naval version of the RAF's T Mk 7, it was fitted with a tail hook and stressed to withstand deck landings on aircraft carriers if required. The nose was also modified to include a fixed searchlight in order to be easily spotted during operations.

The waiting ground crew assisted me to strap into the ejector seat ensuring that the seat straps were as tight as possible. It was a very telling moment when my Flying Helmet was fitted and the two safety pins were removed from the ejector seat and placed in a dedicated holder on the inside of the cockpit. I was now sitting on a live fully armed ejector seat for the first time in my life.

Brian checked that I was ready and started the Rolls Royce Avon jet engine that quickly rumbled into life and settled down to a relaxed whine. On Brian's instruction I fastened my oxygen mask and started to breathe through the mask.

I didn't find that too easy at first, but soon got used to the sensation and almost forgot about it. There was a sort of eyeball instrument on the panel infront of me which 'winked' at every breath that I took and confirmed that I was receiving the correct amount of oxygen.

Brian went through a number of pre-flight checks, and once again after asking if I was OK, he raised the engine revolutions and we started to taxi out to the start of the runway. The visibility from my seat in the right-hand side of the two-seat cockpit was superb.

As we taxied out, Brian continued with his explanations and briefings. I well remember him telling me that from nought to 100 miles per hour the aircraft was quite quick but that an E-Type Jaguar was probably quicker, but after 100 he said that we had the much quicker ride. He then said, "If anything goes wrong up to about 100 miles per hour, I can probably do an emergency stop on the runway, but after that speed we are committed, and I will take her around and come back for an immediate landing. However if you hear me say Broadway Zero Six Eject Eject, Don't say pardon, because I won't be here!" This was it.

After a few seconds at the end of the runway for final clearance Brian spooled up that wonderful RR Avon engine to full power, then released the brakes and we shot off down that runway very rapidly indeed. Suddenly we were off and climbing hard, out over Ilchester getting ever closer to the seemingly solid light grey clouds over us. I will never forget the involuntary ducking of my head as we punched up through that solid-looking cloud layer into the bright blue skies above. Brian obviously found that quite amusing!

Our progress down through Devon and Cornwall seemed to take no time at all, and soon we were over the sea, passing over the Scillies and out into the Atlantic. With the aid of TACAN navigation equipment, we quickly located HMS Blake and received the instructions from her to fly at several different heights and directional headings. As Brian had earlier explained, after each request was completed and confirmed by us, she would request a new height and heading and again we would comply. This went on for some time before Brian declared that we now needed to head for home as our fuel state was reducing. Almost at that moment I became alarmed by a bright flashing warning on the panel in front of me saying 'Low Fuel'. I pointed it out to Brian and was relieved to hear him say, "Don't worry, that's just to tell me that the long range tanks are getting low, but I've still got the main tanks to use yet!"

Brian had earlier explained to me about how the TACAN navigation system worked, and I had been fascinated to see the range counter indicating the nautical miles distant from Yeovilton increasing as we had flown the route. But I was even more fascinated to see the same instrument now rolling back as we flew back towards our base at Yeovilton.

We were about 15 minutes from landing back when Brian asked if I was OK, and would I like to experience some aerobatics? I was not going to miss that opportunity and of course agreed! At which point he commenced a fast barrel roll, and then pulled up hard into a loop. It was strange looking up to see the green earth above me! My head seemed to weigh a ton, especially if I tried to look to one side because it was very hard to get my head back up again.

All too soon it was time to join the circuit and land back at Yeovilton. My wonderful first flight in an aircraft was over, but I was hooked! It had to happen again.

I had not realised it at the time but my pilot that day, Brian Grant, was the most experienced Hunter pilot in the world, with a total of over 14,000 hours behind him, 8,000 of which were on the Hunter He went onto become one of our best airshow display pilots and eventually was the chief pilot flying the Vintage Sea Vixen FAW 2, now owned and managed by the RN Historic Flight. I was truly privileged to fly with him that day. The aircraft that we flew in had originally been built as a single seat Hunter Mk4, WT 702 but it had later been converted into a two seat Hunter TMk8.

To our delight, there was also to be a new member of our family, when baby Esme Jean arrived in early 1978.

By then the new Wincanton by-pass had opened and overnight had turned the town centre from being a dirty bottleneck into a much more pleasant place. However, in mid March that year we had a most unusual incident.

Despite it now being early spring, the weather had turned very cold, and as the day wore on it had started to snow quite heavily. At about 6.30 I walked the 30 yards or so across to my house and noted that the snow was already quite deep, but didn't really give it much thought. Then at about 10.30, my phone rang and it was 249 Bonham ringing from the station and asking for me to come over to see him.

I said something to the effect that I was just going to bed, and he replied, "I really do think that you'd better come over Sarge!"

There was something in his voice that warned me that there was definitely a problem and so I went over immediately. By now the snow had been falling steadily for some hours, and until I stepped outside I had not realised that it had got as bad as it was.

When I entered the station I was amazed to find it was literally full of women! Roy explained that they were a Women's Institute group from somewhere near Okehampton in Devon. They had earlier been on a coach trip to the Ideal Homes exhibition in London, and were at the time on their way home, when their coach had run into a snow drift and had become stuck. The snow was now so deep and drifting, that it had closed the new by-pass. Their coach was going nowhere now, and so Roy with the assistance of two of the others on duty, had used their cars to ferry 35 women and the coach driver back to my station. Little did I know it then, but the group were going to be camping out on emergency mattresses for three days and nights in my parade room!

Luckily, we had an emergency store which contained about a dozen mattresses and blankets, and by trudging around the town we managed to get enough to ensure that they all could lie on my parade room floor. Our wives managed to cook up food etc., and make sandwiches, tea and coffee, etc. The coach driver bedded down in my office.

All of the section's officers and myself spent much of the next few days outside scrambling over huge snow drifts, prodding into the snow, fearful that motorists might still be trapped in the large numbers of abandoned cars. Luckily, everyone was fine and there were no casualties.

After that first heavy snow storm, the weather did improve, but the storm had been so severe that the deep drifts took three days to melt to the point where the A303 could reopen again. Our plight and that of my stranded ladies did feature on several news items.

One bit of that adventure I will never forget! It is a bit indelicate, but nevertheless true. My station was stocked with enough items like toilet paper etc. to last 11 men for about a year. That group of ladies exhausted my stock of toilet rolls in 48 hours! As a result I had to go begging for fresh stocks around the town.

Later that year, PC 172 Mike Stanton moved from Templecombe to become a detective on another division. The move left the detached beat station at Templecombe vacant and PC, I shall call him Smith (not his real name) moved from Wincanton into the vacancy. Smith was a happy sort of individual but he was a bit of a 'chancer', and regrettably his driving of police vehicles did cause me some concern.

This issue came to a head one day when Smith's police van was in the workshops for minor repairs. As a result he had requested permission to use the sergeant's car instead on his van on routine enquiries. I had reluctantly agreed, but was later dismayed to receive a message from the control room to the effect that Smith was reporting having been in a road accident in a lane near Templecombe.

I used a spare vehicle to drive to the scene and found my car with its nose firmly planted in a roadside tree. I approached Smith and immediately accused him of careless driving. His reply was, "It's not my fault, Sarge, A fox ran across in front of me and I instinctively swerved and hit the tree." I replied to the effect that I didn't believe him and he said, "It's true Sarge, I hit it, it's there by the front wheel."

For a few brief moments my anger subsided, but then his luck ran out, for I prodded the obviously dead fox with my boot. It was solid. I turned on him saying, "What's going on, rigor mortis doesn't set in that quickly!"

I touched the fox and it was freezing cold! There then followed a heated discussion with the now very crestfallen constable and I accompanied him back to his section house where I found two more frozen foxes in a deep freeze in his shed.

Clearly this was a matter that had to be reported at a higher level, not least of which was yet more damage to a police vehicle. Under normal circumstances, Smith was a good and industrious constable with a good nose for detecting crime, and so it was finally decided that he should return to a divisional station where his driving skills were less essential. He was replaced by PC Woods.

1978 had been an exciting and testing year for me. I was now regularly performing duty in Yeovil as an acting inspector and gathering still more valuable experience. Sadly, the year was about to end with the most horrific and dreadful incident of my entire police career.

Christmas Eve 1978 was at first very much like any other day. I was catching up on the paperwork in the police station, when just before lunch the control room rang to say that they were sending several units to a reported serious road accident on the A30 just to the east of Henstridge crossroads. It sounded bad so I decided to attend myself.

I was one of the first to arrive and was immediately faced with a horrific scene. A green Triumph Herald estate car was in the road with its entire roof peeled back like a banana skin. Seated in the driver's seat of the car was what appeared from clothing worn, to be the body of a female. She had sustained horrific head injuries, and even to my untrained eye she was quite obviously dead. Worst still, in the back seat of the car were two other much younger females also having suffered catastrophic head injuries. One was also deceased and the other very seriously injured.

Ambulances and a local doctor had also now arrived, as had specialist police road traffic officers. I appointed one of the experienced traffic officers to be the investigating officer, and set about making immediate enquiries. It was evident that a second car was also involved, a blue Ford Corsair which was now stationary some yards to the rear of the Triumph Herald and facing in the opposite direction. It transpired that the Ford had been travelling at some speed and on encountering a humped back bridge had literally taken off, landing on the roof of the Triumph which had been approaching from the opposite direction.

Whilst I was generally supervising the scene and locating any witnesses etc., I was approached by a local resident who informed me that the now deceased driver of the Triumph was a local lady who was the grandmother of the two young girls in the back of the car. She was the long-term carer of both girls. She then added that about an hour earlier she had been with the lady who had spoken on the telephone to her son in London. He was the father of the two young girls and he had by now left London to drive down to Henstridge to spend Christmas with his family.

I realised immediately that it was going to be my unpleasant task to break the news to him, that Christmas was going to be over for him this year, and probably for many more years to come.

I will never forget standing by the front door of a little cottage and seeing him come through the wicket garden gate carrying many wrapped and colourful presents. It's strange to relate but the one little thing that helped a tiny bit was that as he approached I saw a Round Table badge on his lapel, and I knew that I would not have any difficulty in organising immediate support for him in the days to come.

The very youngest daughter had initially been taken by ambulance to Yeovil Hospital but had very quickly been sent to Frenchay Hospital in Bristol where they specialised in head injuries. I arranged for him to be conveyed by fast patrol car to Frenchay, and took the decision to accompany him. The accident scene and the police enquiry were well underway by specialist traffic officers and so my presence there was no longer important.

Sadly, our efforts were in vain and his youngest daughter died soon after our arrival at Frenchay. Arrangements were made to accommodate him there overnight and I returned very sadly to Wincanton and my family. Christmas day was a dreadful day for me too and also my own family who tried hard to make me a little happier. But it took quite a while before I could smile again.

Round Table were outstanding, and ensured that their fellow member was properly looked after for many weeks and that he was constantly given support. I grew quite close to him for a while, but he eventually decided to leave England and moved abroad.

I threw myself back into my work, but even today over 40 years later I do sometimes find myself thinking back to that harrowing scene. I coped with it, I had to, it was my job. And anyway it was long before the concept of post-traumatic incident counselling was introduced. In my day, you accepted that things like that came with the job, and you were expected to get on with it.

However, I do find myself getting very impatient today when I hear young officers complaining that they were not properly prepared to deal with such things, and in some cases even trying to sue their force for not preparing them adequately. My attitude remains, 'If you take the Queen's shilling you have to get on with the job whatever that means!'

The whole family were by now enjoying our life in Wincanton. Paula had found a number of friends after joining Ladies Circle, the wives and partners side of Round Table, Julie and Jeremy had settled into the primary school, and little Esme was growing quickly. The only thing that was causing me concern was the low pay that police officers were receiving at the time. By then I had been a sergeant for five years, yet I was very much aware that the local milk roundsman was receiving about the same as I was. There was certainly very little spare cash for holidays and days out with the family.

The service was losing officers quickly, even my section was affected. PC 1775 Trevor Thomas resigned to take up another better paid career in civilian life in Dorset.

By 1975, the situation in regard to police pay had become so critical that experienced officers were leaving in droves. Even more seriously, recruitment levels had fallen way below the level of resignations. The service was in a desperate crisis. Home Secretary Merlyn Rees decided to appoint Judge Edmond Davies to hold a commission of enquiry into police pay and conditions. His report, published in 1978, highlighted a serious problem with the way police pay had been calculated in the past, and recommended an immediate increase in police pay in the order of 45%. Furthermore, the report recommended that in future police officers should be identified as holding a particular position in the top ten recognised professions in the UK, and that their pay should be automatically calculated annually in order to keep them in that now recognised position, without the need for protracted pay negotiations. By promoting that single recommendation, Lord Edmund Davies ensured that police pay and conditions were guaranteed and conflict-free for decades to come.

One Monday early in 1979, I was as usual prosecuting a number of cases before Wincanton Magistrates Court. The chair was Mrs Montgomery assisted by Mrs Hobhouse and Capt Cunningham.

The last case was that of a young naval lieutenant who had been involved in a road traffic accident whilst driving his Triumph GT6 sports car. His car had impacted with the rear of a Jaguar Mk2, which in turn had struck the rear of a Rolls Royce. The quality of the vehicles involved and the extent of the damage amounted to a very expensive shunt!

On the face of it, it had appeared to be a classic case of driving without due care and attention, and as a result Lt Tarver had subsequently been summoned to appear before Wincanton Magistrates Court.

I prosecuted the case in the normal manner, calling witnesses etc., setting out the case for the prosecution. Lt Tarver was clearly a highly educated individual and presented a very technical defence based on physics. He set out to prove that the kinetic energy generated by his relatively lightweight Triumph GT6 was not sufficient to propel 2 tons of Jaguar Mk2 into the back of the Rolls Royce causing significant damage, and therefore he suggested that the Jaguar had struck the Rolls Royce moments before he hit the rear of the Jaguar.

Obviously I could not accept his version of events, but privately thought that he had run a brilliant defence! The magistrates retired to consider their verdict and I was not surprised when they returned and declared that there was sufficient doubt in their minds to find the defendant Lt Alan Tarver "not guilty".

It was the end of the case list for that day, and the court had now finished its business. Capt Cunningham beckoned me over to the bench and said, "That young lieutenant, ask him is he Tarver GM?" I thought that a bit odd, after all, his name was Alan, but nevertheless did as Capt Cunningham had requested. To my surprise the young lieutenant replied to the effect that yes, he was Tarver GM! Then it dawned on me, the GM stood for George Medal, the highest award for gallantry that this country can award in peacetime.

On confirming that fact to the bench, they immediately declared business over for the day, and invited the young lieutenant to their retiring room for tea. Case concluded!

It was now time for another twist in my career, for suddenly I received a telephone call from Chief Superintendent Taylor in Yeovil, instructing me to report to force headquarters in Bristol the following morning for an interview with Chief Constable Kenneth Steele.

Dennis Taylor was not one for playing games, and he made it quite plain to me that the reason that I was going to see the chief constable was because that I was to be promoted to the rank of inspector. I had been performing duty for quite some time as an acting inspector in Yeovil and knew that things had gone well. The only mystery now was where I was to be posted!

I hoped that it might be to Taunton, but feared that it might be Bridgwater or even Frome, neither of which I was looking forward to.

My appointment was for 10.30 am and as usual Kenneth Steele's diary was running like clockwork, for I was shown into his office in Old Bridewell Bristol at exactly 10.30! His immediate words were, "Sergeant Allinson, it is my intention to promote you to the rank of inspector, and to post you to the city of Bath, are there any real or personal reasons why I should not do that?" My immediate response was, "No sir, thank you sir." And he smiled, shook my hand and said, "Come and sit over here," pointing to some chairs around a small table. He then talked to me for about 20 minutes about his favourite subject, leadership!

I listened to every word, for Ken Steele was himself an outstanding leader, and one who even today, long after his death, I admire. He was a true leader of men.

His final remark, "Now, it's about time that you bought your own house my boy," came as a bit of a surprise, because in the past I had requested permission on at least three occasions to do just that, and had always been refused. Oh well.

When I returned to Wincanton later that day to tell Paula and my family, I could tell that their delight for me personally was tinged with regret for we all realised that our happy times at Wincanton were coming to an end.

Obviously one of my first actions was to arrange an appointment with the chief superintendent of Bath Division. He was none other than George Mathews, the then chief superintendent of police in Yeovil, when I first decided on a career in the police service. He had subsequently moved to take over the Bath Division, which not so many years ago had been a police force in its own right.

He made me most welcome and explained the way the division was organised. He also briefed me on some of the problems that I would experience working on and in a division that was still more than a little resentful of the way its once proud city police force had been disbanded following the countrywide force amalgamations in the mid 1960s, and forced to join the Somerset Force thus becoming just a division of the Somerset and Bath Force. Even now, some 12 years after that amalgamation, many of the original Bath city men still hankered after the old days.

I would be one of four inspectors each in charge of a 'Group' comprising of two sergeants and about ten constables. Each group worked together on an eight-hour shift covering the normal 6-2, 2-10, and 10-6 shifts. They were supplemented by a small number of residential beat officers spread over the city suburbs. By now female officers had ceased to be organised into a separate section, and therefore each group had several female officers on its strength.

It was emphasised that my transfer to Bath Division could not be delayed as the vacancy had been held for some time. They were aware that the question of my accommodation would take a while to resolve as I needed to buy a house, and so I was once again expected to take up temporary lodgings in the city until my own accommodation was found.

The late 70s was a difficult time to arrange mortgages, but I discovered that some building societies did give preference to professional people in my position who were having to move for job-related reasons. I applied and was very pleased to learn that I could borrow as much as £14,000 to buy our first home. Sadly, I very quickly learned that Bath was not the sort of city that had many houses for sale at under £20,000. This was not going to be so easy.

The next task was to visit the force tailor because of course I now had to be issued with an officer's uniform, very different to the one I had worn up until now!

St Stephen's Church, Charlton Musgrove

Our Quarters were in the roof between the Chimneys.

Where I played usually alone

Chantmarle!

My Police Station at Wincanton 1975.
Now a Funeral Parlour!

1st ever flight 5th August 1976. © Robin Walker

Image Gallery **107**

The Launch Day for Western Counties Air Operations Unit (WCAOU)

The First Aircraft we owned!

The lock Up at Castle Cary

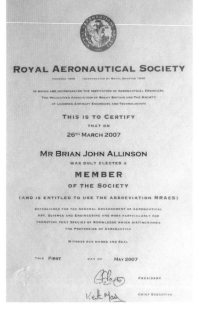

Membership of Royal Aeronautical Society. March 2007

Cut off by Fire. 2015 The Etang De Thau Meze France.

10

An Inspector in Bath

The actual transfer to Bath Division happened quite quickly and in less than three weeks from actually seeing the chief constable I was reporting for work at the police station in Manvers Street, Bath.

This time there was no settling in period like I had when I first went to Weston-super-Mare on promotion to sergeant five years earlier. This time I started with my group on early turn and was expected to get up to speed quickly. I soon found that whilst at Wincanton I was very much in charge, now as a very junior 'senior officer' it felt like I was once again quite a small cog in a much bigger wheel.

The group system of operational deployment meant an immediate return to the full eight-hour shift system of earlies, lates and nights, something that I hadn't done for several years. I didn't find it very easy at first. The first early turn also caused me some concern in an unexpected way! I had arranged to take my breakfast break at around 8.30 am and went up to the canteen where I was aware that the kitchen was able to supply a cooked breakfast if required. I ordered a breakfast and sat down to read my paper when I was approached by a member of the staff who said, "Excuse me sir, but you really aught to be in the officers' mess, not in here." Feeling somewhat embarrassed, I did as she suggested, and had my breakfast in splendid isolation. There was no one else in the mess. I did not like that and protested later to the admin chief inspector. He agreed with me that it was an outdated practise left over from the old city force days. The mess remained as a room but was hardly ever used after that.

The city of Bath was a great place to police. It was busy and interesting, but not manic like I knew that Bristol could be. The only issue was actually getting around. Being very old, the centre of the city was narrow and there were many small alleys containing small shops and businesses. It was of course a tourist magnet and when on foot you could hear so many different languages and dialects. I quickly learned that the best way of supervising my police officers on foot patrol, was to be on foot myself. That also assisted me to rapidly become familiar with the main areas.

One day I was patrolling in company with a young constable near the Orange Grove, a popular tourist spot close to the Abbey. It was famous for floral displays and was looking especially lovely that day. We were approached by a group of about ten American tourists who told us that they would like to take our pictures in front of the floral display. I agreed, and stood with the constable waiting for them to take the pictures. It soon became apparent that they were concerned about something, because there was a lot of discussion going on. Suddenly, one of them came over to me saying, "Gee Lieutenant, we don't really want you in the picture, we only want the proper policeman with the pointed hat!"

It seemed that being an officer had its disadvantages too.

During the summer months especially, Bath was a beautiful city, its parks and gardens were very well tended and its central areas were always featuring some magnificent floral displays. It was a real pleasure to be able to carry out my duties on foot, and to talk with visitors from all over the world. It was a happy city too, and even though there were many pubs and clubs clustered around the centre, there was very little trouble, compared with other towns and cities of a similar size.

Chief Supt George Matthews retired soon after my arrival in Bath and was replaced by Acting Chief Supt Hugo Pike. Widely experienced, he was to prove significant in my later development in the service.

From my point of view, the only disadvantage of the posting to Bath was the cost of property within the city limits. Paula and I quickly realised that our absolute limit of £18,000 with which to buy a house was not going to find us one in Bath, so we had started to look beyond and towards Bristol.

We finally found a small semi-detached three-bedroom house in Longwell Green. It was brand new, having just been built by the developer Wimpy on their new California farm estate. It was marketed as a basic starter home, having single glazed windows, and no central heating, but at least it was going to be ours, and our family would be together again! So we agreed to buy. At least now my family could join me in a new adventure in our life.

Working in Bath continued to be interesting, certainly never dull. The river added an element that I had not experienced before. Sadly people had a tendency to fall in, very often as a result of drinking too much alcohol. Also on a warm night the slowly flowing water could appear inviting, and so a few jumped in deliberately, seeking to cool off. Sadly the sudden shock of entering the unexpectedly cold water often caused a rapid loss of consciousness. In addition the weir, close to the famous Pulteney Bridge, had a nasty undertow and was deeper than summer bathers expected.

The Pulteney weir was always the first place we looked when reports came in of missing people believed to have fallen in the river.

Whilst the Bath city posting was extremely valuable from an experienced gained point of view, I didn't find it very challenging and found myself hoping for something new to come along. And it did!

Hugo Pike had called me to his office one day and we talked for a while about my experiences as a force firearms coordinator. I could tell that he was leading up to something. Finally he reminded me that much of the land between Norton Radstock and Keynsham was Duchy Of Cornwall land under the stewardship of Prince Charles, the Prince of Wales. In a few weeks' time the Prince was intending to visit several of his tenanted farms in the area, and it had been decided that I would be the local senior police officer to accompany the Prince on the visit. I was to make contact with the local Duchy of Cornwall Office in Bath and through them the Prince of Wales' personal protection officer. It would be necessary for both of us and several Duchy officials to walk the intended route and to meet and brief the tenant farmers that the Prince would be meeting on the day.

The dry run took place about two weeks later, starting from Newton St Loe near Bath. The walk took quite a while and encompassed four different farms, ending close to Queen Charlton near Keynsham. We spent quite a while with each farmer, briefing them on the sort of questions that the Prince might ask them, checking the facilities available at the location, and guiding what suitable refreshments might be offered. I remember clearly that it was emphasised that the Prince would not drink alcohol on such a visit, but did appreciate a glass of Shloer non-alcoholic fruit juice.

I spent some time in discussion with the Prince's personal protection officer who briefed me on what was expected of me should any unforeseen incident occur. Quite obviously, his primary task was the protection of the Prince of Wales. My task as the local officer was to provide any necessary back-up but also to use my local knowledge to establish a safe route away from the incident giving cause for alarm.

On the day of the visit I had been briefed to wear a smart casual jacket and trousers, and the force had issued me with an oiled Barbour jacket outer coat, which easily concealed my force-issued Smith & Wesson Model 10 .38 Special revolver. I was confident in my ability to carry out the task, but slightly nervous on my first assignment of this type.

In the event, the visit went well. The weather was kind to us. Sunny but not too hot, and each of the planned visits proved to be happy and pleasant occasions. The Prince was clearly very much at ease with his tenant farmers and enjoyed asking lots of animal husbandry and arboreal questions. Most of which were way above my head.

I thoroughly enjoyed the experience and made a lot of valuable contacts for the future.

Then, in the autumn of 1980, Hugo Pike asked me how I would like a trip to Japan! He went on to explain that he was in Rotary International, a worldwide fellowship of businessmen dedicated to promoting international peaceful understanding. His Rotary district was proposing to organise a six-week 'Group Study Exchange' with a Rotary District in Central Japan. It was intended that the outgoing team from the southwest of England would comprise of five young men from differing occupations who would study their own occupations whilst in Japan. Later the same year, a Japanese team would then come to southwest England in order to study their occupations.

He, Hugo Pike, was prepared to recommend me to his club, the Bath City Rotary Club, as worthy of being their nomination to the district as a member of the team. There followed two local interviews at which I was successful and I was allocated a final district interview in Wells, Somerset, at the end of October 1980. I prepared carefully for this final interview because there was clearly a lot riding on it.

Then just over two weeks before the date set I suddenly began to feel very unwell whilst at work. I just about managed to drive home, but as soon as I got there I went straight to bed. The following day I was even worse and a very worried Paula sent for the doctor. The diagnosis was mumps! Never pleasant, but even worse for a 35-year-old male.

I really don't remember much about the next ten days but I eventually got a little better, although was still confined to bed. It was obvious by then that there was no way that I was going to be able to make the Wells interview so with a heavy heart I telephoned the Rotary organiser to inform them that I would have to withdraw. He was very concerned, but said that as time was pressing they had to resolve the team appointments quickly and could not offer a later date.

However, a day later he phoned back to say that they had organised a telephone conference call, and would I be prepared to be interviewed over the phone? Obviously I agreed to the suggestion and a new time was set on the original date.

The interview itself was relatively easy, and consisted mainly of questions to establish my level of knowledge about the British governmental system, our history and also about the southwest of England, its cities and important businesses, etc.

A few days later I received a letter to tell me that I had been selected, and would be flying out to Japan in early March 1981. Wow!

Our team covered a wide mix of experience. Our ages spanned from 26 to 35, and comprised of a water board engineer, a farmer, a quarry manager, a building society manager and a police officer. Now we had to learn to work together as a team on presentations, to give talks about our occupations and the part of England that we were from. Our team leader, John Mitchell, was an experienced Rotarian from Yeovil. We had three months to prepare for the trip, perfect our individual presentations, collect small presents for our hosts and choose a team uniform. In the end that bit was simple, dark navy blazers and grey flannels were chosen!

We all worked hard and were quickly working as a team, then suddenly it was time to go, it was early March 1981. We met at Heathrow and boarded our Cathay Pacific 747 jumbo jet bound for Hong Kong. The flight was 14 hours long and seemed to go on for ever, but all the time the excitement was growing. I knew that the approach and landing at Kai Tak Airport Hong Kong was quite famous in aviation circles and so I had made sure that I had a window seat. I was not disappointed. It was spectacular! The aircraft made a tight turn around some rocky high ground and then appeared to be flying along a commercial road leading to the runway itself. I could see people only a few feet below us calmly carrying on with their shopping! We landed with a slight bump and then the brakes came on very hard as the captain needed to stop the heavy aircraft quickly. The end of the runway was jutting out over the sea, so overshooting was not advisable!

The next stage of our long journey to Japan involved a six-hour stopover in Hong Kong, before we could board another aircraft for the flight via Taipei to Narita Airport in Japan.

Six hours in a very crowded and noisy airport was not attractive so we decided to make the most of the stopover and explore Kowloon. Our taxi dropped us near the waterfront and the adventure was underway! It was so hot and humid that a nice cool beer soon became a priority and we found a bar overlooking the harbour.

I will never forget that ice cold San Miguel lager that we had there – it was fantastic! Our version of the film Ice Cold in Alex.

Our few hours in Kowloon passed all too quickly and very soon we were back at Kai Tak Airport ready for the next part of our journey to Japan. We were again flying with Cathay Pacific, but this time our aircraft was a Lockheed Tristar, smaller than the Jumbo 747 but still big enough to be regarded as a 'heavy' or large passenger aircraft. It was powered by three powerful Rolls Royce engines.

The take-off out of Hong Kong was spectacular to say the least. When we had taken off from Heathrow, the big jumbo had surged into the air and had climbed away steadily. The Tristar seemed to hurtle down the runway and then leaped into the air climbing at a very steep angle. So steep was the angle, that from my position halfway down the passenger cabin, I seemed to be looking upwards whilst merely looking along the aircraft cabin. Despite being an aircraft enthusiast, I had forgotten that Kai Tak Airport was one of the most difficult airfields to operate into and out of, because of the rocky and high terrain that surrounded it. The steep take-off was very necessary for safety. The rest of the flight was otherwise uneventful, and after about two hours we landed at Taipei, the capital city of Taiwan. This was also a refuelling stop, so we had to vacate the aircraft whilst it was refuelled. There were a lot of grim-looking armed guards about, and I was quite glad to re-board the aircraft after about 30 minutes. Off again, this time an easier take-off.

After another four hours we landed at Narita Airport, Japan. Narita was then still very new and officially the new airport for Tokyo, despite being about 100 kms from the capital city. We were met by an official greeting party of Japanese Rotarians. The shaking of hands and the bowing seemed to go on for ages, as did the exchanging of business cards (maeshi). We had learned the correct form of holding the proffered card in both hands, and reading it whilst bowing at the same time.

We boarded a specially chartered minibus and travelled with our hosts into Central Tokyo to our beautiful and quite famous hotel, The Okura. It was then one of the most important hotels in the city and frequented by many famous stars and politicians.

By this time we were very tired and after a couple of nightcaps we headed for our very luxurious rooms. This trip was starting to feel very good indeed!

The Rotary organisers had planned for us to spend two days in Tokyo, both in order to recover from our long flight and to acclimatise ourselves to a new culture. They had arranged for us to visit the Diet (the seat of government in Japan, the equivalent of the Palace of Westminster in London). The imposing building was beautifully designed and built using grey granite. It had been built to withstand quite severe earthquakes. We learned that Japan was relatively unstable geologically, and as a result suffered from quite frequent but mainly very minor earth tremors. All buildings that had been built in recent years had to be designed and built to resist the effects of earthquakes. We also visited the famous Ginza District with many clubs, restaurants and shops.

Tokyo was teaming with people, yet unlike many large western cities it felt a very safe place to be. It was also remarkably clean, there was very little rubbish in the street.

Our acclimatisation complete, we soon found ourselves headed out of Tokyo to the northwest to Gunma prefecture, one of the two Japanese districts that had funded our visit. Gunma was located in the central mountainous region of the country. Its main city was Maebashi. The very famous Nikko shrine area was close by. We were variously accommodated with host Japanese families, usually two of us at each location. Each morning and also in the afternoon we would be visiting different factories or large commercial centres.

Then at lunchtime we would be expected to give our now well-rehearsed presentations at a combined meeting of several Rotary clubs. This routine was almost endless and quite tiring.

Each team member had been promised a period of vocational attachments designed to encourage greater understanding of how their occupations differed in the Japanese environment. Accordingly It had been arranged for me to have two attachments to two different police forces during my visit. To assist with those attachments I had been asked to take my police inspector's uniform with me in order that citizens would recognise me as a visiting police officer.

My first attachment was to Maebashi Police, and I was driven around the city by the senior superintendent of the area. I was fascinated by the way the Japanese police service was organised. They had positioned themselves much closer to the public they served than the British system allowed for.

The Japanese system was based on the Koban. The Koban being a very small police station staffed by only four to six officers, and covering a very small area. In contrast, the British policing model was tending to move towards much bigger, almost fortress-like police stations, covering greater areas and grouping a significant number of police officers in one place.

In the Koban system, each officer was responsible for a particular street and was expected to maintain accurate records of each family living in his street. He would arrange to visit each family at least once a year, and to sit down with them making notes of who lived there, how old they were, where they worked, what car they owned, and what insurance company covered it, etc. Here we would reject such a practice as 'big brother' but there the attitude was reversed. The police were there to help them and to assist them in many ways.

The superintendent assured me that if the police officer did not make his routine call for any reason he would receive a complaint to the effect that 'Why are you ignoring me? What have I done wrong?'

Crime was at a very low level, almost non-existent to the ordinary family. To have a family member commit a crime of dishonesty was to inflict a huge disgrace on the whole family and the person involved was almost certain to be disowned. That is not to say that crime didn't exist, but it was invariably white collar crime, such as company fraud etc.

Of course, crime did exist, but it was almost exclusively the business of organised criminal gangs otherwise known as the Yakusa. Whilst being driven through city suburbs one day we passed a very gaudily decorated shop front. I commented on the bright decorations and my superintendent friend said, "Oh that's the headquarters of the Red Triangle gang!" (not the real name). I expressed surprise that they should seek to advertise their HQ, and was then even more surprised at his explanation. He explained that being a member of a gang was not in itself a crime, it was just a fellowship or grouping of a number of men. They ran the gambling casinos, the prostitution and the drugs supply. If an ordinary person wanted to avail themselves of whatever the gangs offered, then they needed to know where to find them. In short, the gangs needed to advertise their presence, hence the bright shop front!

So this was a huge cultural difference. In Japan, crime was not acceptable to the common man to any great extent. And recognising that fact, the criminal side of society tended to keep their activities away from the ordinary citizen. The gangs, however, had found different ways of making their profitable but illegal activities available to those who wanted them.

Another surprise came when I commented on the very low numbers of female officers available to the police. My superintendent replied, "We do have a small number of them for dealing with problems involving children and a very few female prisoners, but not for normal policing, and anyway where would they sleep?" That seemed a very strange answer until he showed me the top floor of the police station which had a lot of sleeping mats on the floor. I realised that crime was so low that the police force of this big city only actually patrolled the streets until about 1 am, and then retired to bed very much as our firefighters on night shifts in England did. They were of course immediately available should their services be needed. This was an entirely different police world.

Later our team moved further across the main island of Japan to the northern coastal city of Niigata. Once again we had several weeks of giving talks and presentations on England, visiting factories and power stations, and appearing on TV, etc. Niigata was much bigger than Maebashi and I spent some time with the police anti-riot training school. They were very well trained but actually were not used very much. However, I picked up a number of points that would later help me back in England.

My main police attachment in Niigata was to the roads policing unit, and once again this was to prove very different to my policing experiences in England.

The roads policing unit was mainly tasked with accident prevention and anti-speeding activities. To do this they had introduced what would seem to us to be a ridiculous initiative of persuading all car owners to fit radar detectors in their cars. But actually the idea was extremely effective! Early each morning the unit would place out a large number of dummy or blind radar transmitters interspersed with a smaller number of real radar speed cameras. As a result, drivers were constantly receiving warnings on their detectors and slowing down at each warning received. There was no way of telling which were genuine radar traps and which were not. The locations of the genuine traps were changed each day.

This was a truly effective way of making modern technology work for the safety of everyone, and showed that the police were not merely interested in punishing errant drivers.

Five weeks into the visit to Japan, the team was really feeling the strain. It had been a wonderful experience and the organisation that went into it by the Rotary Clubs in Japan had been faultless.

We had noticed quite early on that as the team was passed on from one host Rotary Club to the next, so too was an impressively bulky file. The file was obviously a report into us, our apparent likes and dislikes, etc. Obviously we were never shown it and in any event as it would have been written or typed in Japanese we wouldn't be able to read it. However, one thing was obviously very clearly set out in the report and that was the fact that we could withstand a prodigious amount of alcohol!

At this point I must emphasise that we were not in any way heavy drinkers, but it was evident that the average Japanese person could only take a very small amount of alcohol before the effects became very apparent. Whereas we were never adversely affected. However, with this ability to withstand drink being very clearly reported in our log, at almost every occasion when we arrived at a new location we were expected to undergo a trial of drinking skills with the local drinking team! The scenario was always the same, we were seated cross legged at one side of a long and very low table. The opposition were seated opposite us grinning evilly. Then the bottles of Kirin beer would arrive and were quickly drunk, then a new batch and then another. Soon we changed to hot saki. We would be having a great time, but very soon the opposition were looking quite unhappy, giggling stupidly and often falling over. That is how our reputation came about – we were never beaten or affected in any way. They could not get over it.

Finally we moved to the old Imperial City of Kyoto and spend a wonderful last few nights in a traditional Japanese ryokan or hotel. We were also given a private viewing of the old Imperial Palace and grounds. The palace was once the emperor's palace in the days before Tokyo became the capital city. It was fabulous!

Then seven weeks after we left England we started our long return journey home. However, we had planned a two-day stopover in Hong Kong on the way home and enjoyed exploring Hong Kong Island and its famous peak.

My family were waiting to meet me at Heathrow when we got home. The trip had been a great experience and I had learned a great deal about public speaking and presentations, etc. but it was even better to be home with my young family again.

On my return to Bath I discovered that Chief Supt Hugo Pike had been successful in his bid to become the deputy commandant of the Police Staff College at Bramshill House near Basingstoke. He had been replaced by Ch Supt Alan Thackway who I had not previously worked with. He was obviously experienced and quickly earned my respect. The only problem I had with him was that for some reason he thought my name was Malcolm and not Brian. No matter how many times I reminded him that I was Brian, he always referred to me as Malcolm. I was told later that he was a fan of a well-known footballer Malcolm Alison, which is what probably caused the problem.

One day he requested that I accompany him to the detached section station at Radstock, a few miles south of Bath. Radstock section was a large semi-rural section twinned with Keynsham Section to the west of Bath. The two sections formed a separate county sub division on Bath Division. On the way there, Alan explained that he was not happy that the section was working to the standard that he believed it should. He recognised that although bigger in population numbers, Radstock was not unlike my old Wincanton section and so he valued my thoughts on how to improve it.

We spent about three hours there, talking to the two sergeants and several of the men. They were all experienced and good officers. They clearly knew their patch well and there was no reason why they should not work well as a team, but...

On the way back to Bath, Alan asked me what I thought the problem was. My response was, "I think it's a leadership issue!" "Oh, how so?" To me it was plain and simple. There were two sergeants there, both good and experienced sergeants, but in their own ways very different. So who was in charge? My thoughts were that in any organisation, be it large or small, someone has to be in charge, the leader. No wonder the team was not delivering! Alan said, "I thought you would say that, that's why I took you along!"

Two weeks later I learned that I was being transferred to Radstock as its first inspector in charge.

Radstock section was part of the Keynsham subdivision of Bath Division. The subdivision was commanded by a chief inspector with inspectors in direct supervision of stations at Keynsham and Radstock.

I found Radstock to be a great posting. It was much busier to police than Wincanton had been. The area was once a mining community, the people were tough and not afraid to make a point if they felt strongly about something. The officers stationed there were of the same stock and were very much part of the community.

However much as I was enjoying Radstock, my career was about to take yet another turn as another great opportunity presented itself.

There had been one inspector's post in the force that was almost guaranteed to result in eventual promotion to the rank of chief inspector. Conversely, it also had the potential to get you condemned to a life in the Tower of London if things didn't go well. The post was called 'The inspector special events', however the holder was also the staff officer to the assistant chief constable (operations).

The current holder of the post was Inspector Mike Jenkinson. He had been in post for three years and, true to form, had just been promoted to chief inspector on a Bristol Division.

Naturally, I was very interested in that now vacant post, and in the knowledge that my recent visit to the Duchy of Cornwall estates had gone well, I let it be known that I was interested. My expression of interest was taken up very quickly and almost immediately I was invited to appear before Chief Superintendent 'Tug Wilson' of the Support Services Division. He had a reputation of being a real tough cookie, but one who was great to work for. He gave me the toughest 20-minute interview that I had ever endured, but then suddenly grinned and shook my hand. He informed me that he was going to recommend my appointment as the inspector special events, and as staff officer to Assistant Chief Constable Operations Walter (Wally) Girvan.

Royal Visit

11

The
Inspector
Special
Events

My new role carried with it the responsibility for the planning of all royal and VIP events in the force area, together with other strategic and sporting events requiring additional manpower to be provided from other divisions.

In recognition of the importance of settling into the new role, and of adjusting to the new responsibilities, the handover in this post was always managed closely and almost for the first time in my career I was able to work closely with Mike Jenkinson for at least two weeks. It was a steep learning curve but the role was extensively documented and it soon became evident that there was precedent for most types of visits.

The most frequent and basic task was monitoring the home game fixtures for the two main Bristol football teams. The early eighties was a time of frequent football hooliganism, and as a result the force had evolved a three-tier classification system for both teams. Each match was classified as being of low, medium or high risk, depending on the reputation of the visiting team. Then depending on the risk level I would set the number of task forces to be allocated to the match commander, and in the case of higher risk games the numbers of mounted officers and dog handlers. Finally I would prepare the operational order for signature by the assistant chief constable operations.

The most interesting element of the job, however, were the royal and VIP visits. It quickly became evident that there were more of these visits taking place across the force area than I had realised. Many were low-key semi-private events but each had to be considered against possible threats, and the appropriate level of cover provided. It was at a time when the troubles in Northern Ireland were at their height and the general threat level heightened.

Notification of a proposed royal visit would be sent by the Lord Lieutenant to the ACC Ops, and he would instruct me to commence the planning process. My first action would be to make contact with the Lord Lieutenant, and also the royal or VIP personal protection officer responsible for whoever was making the visit (referred to as the principal).

Following an initial discussion with the Lord Lieutenant concerning the nature of the proposed visit, I would make contact with the principal's PPO, in order to make arrangements for our first meeting and arrange for the vital walk through of the location selected for the visit.

That first meeting with the principal's protection officer would usually involve a senior officer from the force's Special Branch department in order to agree the level of additional protection that the force would need to supply. Following the initial meeting I would then arrange a number of dry runs of the planned visit. These would involve the Traffic Division commander responsible for ensuring a smooth uninterrupted escort for the principal, and usually the divisional commander responsible for the location concerned. The dry runs would involve the recording of the timing of every element of the visit, in order for me to commence the preparation of the required operational order.

The operational order would specify the required manpower element and the extra support needed from specialist departments to supplement the divisional strength. Officers in charge of the various elements of the visit would be identified by name. Nothing would be left to chance.

There were simply too many visits for me to mention them all, but I will reveal a small number mainly to emphasise the importance of remaining flexible in response to unexpected developments.

I well remember a visit by Princess Alexandra to the Bath and West Agricultural Show near Shepton Mallet in Somerset one very hot day in June.

Such visits normally involved the principal arriving at the show ground in a helicopter from the Royal Flight, but it was known that the Princess was not one who liked flying in helicopters. Arrangements had therefore been made for her to fly by a fixed-wing aircraft to RNAS Yeovilton, a few miles south of the showground itself. I had arranged for a small motorcade to be at the Air Station, and we would then escort her through minor roads to the showground. All went well and the plans all ran smoothly until, that is, it was time to take the Princess back to the Air Station.

The motorcade was re-formed and the Princess boarded her limousine as planned and we set off back along the minor country roads towards our destination. I was in my usual place in the lead patrol car, looking through my handheld mirror which allowed me a good view of the principal's car.

Suddenly I saw a regular flashing of the limousine's headlights, usually a sign of a problem.

I stopped the motorcade and walked back to speak to the PPO who grinned at me and said, "It's very hot, the Princess would like an ice cream, do you think we could find one?"

I will never forget the jaw-dropping moment when I brought the motorcade to a halt near a small local shop in the village of Doynton and I got out in my very best uniform and said to the lady behind the counter, "The Princess is very hot, and would love one of your ice creams!" I suspect she told that story for many years after that visit.

When we got to Yeovilton, the VIPs and dignitaries were all lined up to see the Princess off and she went down the line shaking everyone's hand until she got to ACC Girvan, the senior police officer present. She shook his hand and said, "Thank you Mr Girvan for the splendid arrangements, but I know that you personally don't make these plans, and I would like to thank whoever did!" Mr Girvan called me over, and she shook my hand and thanked me most kindly. I now had a new royal favourite!

One dark and very wet late autumn night, I was sitting in the lead car of a small motorcade waiting on the over bridge at Junction 18 of the M4. We were peering out into the darkness searching for the special light that would indicate the approach up the slip road of a royal limousine containing Princess Margaret. I had been advised about six weeks earlier that on this night she would arrive at our location at approximately 5 pm and that we would escort her car to the Royal Crescent Hotel in Bath where she would stay for the night. It was planned that at 6.15 pm she would be driven to the old Green Park railway station in Bath. The station had long been closed as part of the Beeching cuts and had now been converted into a new Sainsbury's supermarket. She would officially open the new store and then be taken to the Theatre Royal in Bath where she would watch a performance by a major ballet company.

This important visit by a major royal was an important one and had been subject to much planning and careful timing. But now she was already about 30 minutes late. The bad weather and heavy traffic on the M4 had seriously delayed her car and the Metropolitan Police Jaguar that was following it. Then at about 5.30 we spotted her car approaching and my motorcade took up station ahead and behind her two cars. We piloted them via Freezing Hill Lane and Lansdown to the Royal Crescent Hotel.

The motorcade pulled up outside the hotel and I witnessed the very small personage of Princess Margaret dressed in a white fur coat alight from the rear of the Rolls Royce and enter the hotel via some revolving doors. Her PPO also entered the hotel after instructing his assistants to go to another hotel where they were staying, and unload their bags. I remained standing on the pavement outside the hotel. Suddenly I was approached by the royal chauffeur who said that his Rolls Royce was very dirty after the run from London and could I get him a bucket and sponge!

I managed to persuade the hotel to provide the necessary items and he started to wash down the offside of the car. By now he was hidden from my view, washing the area by the offside front wheel. I was still standing on the pavement between the car and the entrance to the hotel. Suddenly, I became aware of a small figure dressed in a white fur coat emerging from the revolving door of the hotel. I flung up a salute, snatched open the rear nearside door of the car and Princess Margaret entered and sat down. I closed the door and almost lost my cool! The rule is that when royal bottoms hit the leather in a car, the car moves off. But the chauffeur, unaware of all this, was still washing the wheel, and the PPO and his staff were nowhere to be seen.

I started to call everyone in a loud stage whisper, "She's in the car, She's in the car!" Slowly light dawned and the PPO came rushing out, his assistants arrived too. The chauffeur suddenly realised what had happened and, in jumping up, knocked over his bucket with a loud crash.

I will not forget the look on the face of that little figure on the back seat of the Rolls Royce. She had a broad grin, because she had caught us all out and she knew it! It transpired that she had decided to try and get back as close as possible to the original schedule by cutting short on her rest period in the hotel. Sadly, her PPO had not realised what was happening and he too had been caught out. There were a few red faces in that motorcade as we drove to Sainsbury's. There she opened the store, selected a bottle of Famous Grouse and we went off to the Theatre Royal. The remainder of the visit was uneventful.

A few months later another change of a royal plan was to get me into real trouble with my boss, ACC Walter Girvan. This time the principal was the Princess Royal, Princess Anne. She was making a visit to an opera at the Hippodrome theatre in Bristol. I had done the usual amount of detailed planning and timing, etc. and this time as it involved a senior royal my boss had decided that he would accompany me in the lead car, and would be accompanied by his wife.

We drove to Gatcombe House in Gloucestershire, and then escorted the royal car to the centre of Bristol and the Hippodrome.

The Princess alighted and entered the theatre where she was greeted by the Lord Lieutenant and VIP guests including Mr Girvan who had slipped in ahead of her to be in the guest line-up.

I took the motorcade away for a rest and refreshments during the time that the Princess was watching the opera. At the conclusion of the performance, the Princess would then go backstage to meet the artists and would be accompanied by my boss as the senior police officer present. However, it became clear that the space backstage was extremely limited and he decided to return to the bar area upstairs where the Princess was expected to take her leave before departure back to Gatcombe. I brought the motorcade back to the front of the Hippodrome in plenty of time, and was there ready and waiting for the royal party to come out. Suddenly, about one minute early, I saw Princess Anne and her PPO emerge from the front of the theatre and come towards her car. The chauffeur was on the ball and had the door open in a flash and as soon as she was properly seated the engine started and the car started to move forward. But where was my boss? He was nowhere to be seen! I could not wait, that rule that was broken in Bath was not going to happen again! So I took the motorcade to Gatcombe myself.

We returned to the centre of Bristol, not much before midnight, and there standing outside the Hippodrome with his wife was my boss Walter Girvan. To say that the atmosphere was icy would be an understatement. Neither of them said a word on the journey to their home near Blagdon Lake. But as he got out of the car there was the ominous instruction, "My office, 11 am tomorrow." The Tower of London was looming!

I had already discovered what had gone wrong. After the boss had decided to wait in the bar for the Princess to return to say her goodbyes, she had decided not to return to the bar but leave immediately via the front doors. So he had been left behind and I had quite correctly taken the motorcade back to Gatcombe. But of course rank has its privileges in any disciplined organisation, and so of course the fault was quite clearly mine!

I had the telling off of my life for about 30 minutes. But then his voice softened, he leant down, opened a drawer in his desk and said, "Right, now that's an end to it! Gin and tonic?" He knew that it wasn't my fault, but he had to be seen to take action. It was done and we were colleagues again.

Royal visits were always great, but I suppose the best was always the wonderful Badminton Horse Trials at the beginning of May each year.

It was a major force undertaking, and the manpower requirements were so great that all leave and rest days were cancelled through every division in the force. All of the major royals would be there, staying at the house itself. The force would be required to provide a full armed guard for the entire period of the show.

But it all had to be very carefully stage managed. Several of the royals, but especially the Duke of Edinburgh, hated to see police officers around, and was known to get quite caustic about it. So a big part of my task was to hide them in various locations whilst still ensuring that they were available immediately if needed! But that apart, it was always a great event.

Working with royal visitors was always stressful because of the potential for a terrorist or fanatical attack. However, after the IRA had murdered Lord Louis Mountbatten, the reduction in their incoming financial support meant that an attack was unlikely. However, the risk was multiplied when working with VIP politicians! There you knew that sooner or later an attack was very likely so you could take no chances whatsoever. The only one that I spent any time with was Norman Tebbit and I found him fascinating to talk to. He had a mind as sharp as a razor.

During the three years that I was working as the inspector special events, time seemed to fly by, and there were constantly new lessons to be learned. However, there was one experience that was later to play a significant part in the second half of my career. The frequent need for dry runs etc., especially when planning visits involving several different locations, meant that on occasions I was able to fly in the Queen's helicopter. This was for planning purposes of course, and no royalty would be there. But It did bring firmly to my notice just what wonderful visibility you had from up there at about 500 feet above ground level.

Our finest ever chief constable, Ken Steele, had retired in 1979 after 25 years, firstly as chief of Somersetshire, then Somerset and Bath and since 1974 as chief of Avon and Somerset Constabulary. He finally retired in 1979 and was replaced by Brian Weigh who then left after a relatively short tenure in 1983. No replacement chief had been selected at the time of his departure, and so our long-time deputy chief constable, John Harland, was serving as acting chief constable.

I had just been over to New Bridewell for a routine meeting with Ch Supt Tug Wilson, and was heading back to my office in Old Bridewell when I literally bumped into John Harland who was just coming out of his office. "Ah Allinson," he said. "I want you for a minute, come in!"

I went into his office and he said, "You've done a good job at special events, and I'm promoting you to chief inspector at St George, as soon as your replacement can be found, well done!" We then had a discussion about what he wanted from me at St George.

The station had very recently hit the headlines when the current chief inspector had had a falling out with one of his detectives in a nearby pub and a fracas had ensued. The media had heard of it and disciplinary action had meant moves for both officers. Morale was down and needed to be brought back. He also reminded me that this was going to be a very different sort of posting. He said I had been living 'high on the hog' at special events, but now I was going to experience a very different sort of service. St George, it was said, had been built in 1861, but had not had a penny spent on it since. An exaggeration of course, but as I was to find, not far out!

I went back to my office in a bit of a daze, as this had come as a complete surprise. I telephoned Tug Wilson who I had been with only 30 minutes before and who had said nothing to me about promotion. I said, "Sir, I think that I've just been promoted, did you know?" He replied, "What! No, I haven't been told anything, wait there, don't do anything and I'll come back to you."

Within five minutes the phone rang and it was Tug again. "You're right," he said. "You have been promoted, congratulations!" He went on to explain that the procedure had all gone awry when I had bumped into the DCC outside of his office. He had taken the opportunity to make the promotion before he had been able to speak to Tug. So almost by accident I became the only officer as far as I know to be promoted by an acting chief constable.

There followed a frenetic scramble to identify a replacement for me in Special Events and for me to effect a proper handover. By coincidence, my replacement was identified as Inspector Steve Lucas who had taken over my group in Bath when I left there to go to Radstock. He was following me about!

So now it was time to become second in command at St George Police Station in Bristol.

The Police Staff College, Bramshill | © Geoff Cheshire

12

Chief Inspector St George!

My first impressions of St George Police Station came as a bit of a shock. I knew that it was very old but had expected some modernisation. Yes, it had electric lighting and some hot and cold water, but the walls were rough and just washed over with emulsion. The front office and the parade room were dingy and dark, and the cells looked like something straight out of a Victorian horror film.

Climbing up some bare wooden stairs to the first floor, I found the inspector's office, where the four shift inspectors had a desk each. My office was next door. It was a fairly large room and had an impressive sized desk in the far corner. There was a wooden wardrobe to take my uniform, and a small table against one wall holding several box files.

Finally, in a similar but slightly larger room was the sub-divisional commander's office. Here I met my new boss, Superintendent Roy 'Bogeye' Jones. He welcomed me with great enthusiasm, and despite my alarm at the fabric of the station, I knew that my posting to St George was going to be a happy one!

From day one I got on with Roy Jones very well. He told me what he expected of me, but went out of his way to say that he realised that I had been out of operational policing for some time and he accepted that I would need some time to settle in. In the event, it didn't take that long but there were some adjustments to be made. Firstly, the jump from the rank of inspector to chief inspector was greater than I had realised. If I passed comment on something as an inspector, it was noted but not necessarily carried out immediately. But now I found that I needed to be more careful. On a couple of occasions early on I had commented on something saying, "Perhaps we should..." and then found that they had done it immediately before I had really come to a solid conclusion! I learned that one quickly.

Being from the Victorian age, there was one aspect of the station that I found hilarious. That was the superintendent's loo! On my very first day its presence was indicated to me by Roy Jones, and he proudly said I could use it. It was as you would expect, quite small with one large frosted window. The toilet itself was very old and was flushed with the pull of an old-fashioned chain. The chain then disappeared up through the ceiling. To my amusement, I then discovered that immediately above on the second floor of the building was the typists' general office. The chain emerged through the floor of their office and carried on upwards, finally disappearing into the roof void where the cistern obviously was!

I had a great bunch of group inspectors, John Hodges, an ex-naval petty officer, and Jim Millard had both been inspectors for many years, Tony Blyth, also with many years' service, had started his police career as a cadet. He was always to be seen smoking a cigarette which had a long drooping ash end to it. Brian Roebuck, a strong disciplinarian, was a firm and totally reliable ex-traffic officer. He was an ex-Gloucester Constabulary man. His father had been a police officer before him.

Each of the four inspectors ran a well-balanced team of constables and sergeants, and I very rapidly concluded that the whole sub division took much delight in working together, in order to overcome the almost unique challenges presented by their surroundings.

The rear station yard contained the canteen and small social club which housed the snooker table. Roy Jones would be found there most lunchtimes playing snooker with the two admin sergeants, 'Moggie' Morgan and Larry Tiley.

The yard itself was very small, constructed well before the car was invented. It may have been suitable for the horses once upon a time, but it had too many obstacles for the unwary officer manoeuvring a panda car. We had one or two scrapes there!

As is always the case where a number of officers group together, you will find the characters, and St George was no exception. I will never forget John Bush, 'Bushy' as he was known to everyone. As strong as an ox, he always reminded me of the comic character Desperate Dan. In the canteen I always expected to see him eating cow pie! There were even folk stories about Johny Bush. It was said that he balanced heavy wooden ladders on his chin. I never believed those stories until one quiet afternoon I heard a lot of cheering and clapping from the back yard and so I looked out of the window. There was Bushy, stripped down to his shirtsleeves balancing a heavy wooden ladder vertically on his chin, to the obvious delight of his group. The funny thing about Bushy was that as strong as he was, if he ever caught a cold, it would go straight to his chest and he would be off ill for weeks.

My final memory of Bushy was late one night when the whole station was filled with an agonised bellow and some quite colourful language coming from the male toilets. It transpired that the cleaners had unfortunately placed a caustic block at the front of the toilet pan, Bushy had decided to spend a few quiet moments in there, and a delicate part of his anatomy had come in contact with the block! We all heard about that!

The role of being the chief inspector or deputy sub-divisional commander at St George was quite challenging in that it required a new set of skills. I had already demonstrated that I could handle the wide spectrum of operational duty, but this new role required an ability to think strategically and to plan for the unexpected. 1983 had seen the onset of conflicts with militant miners at various collieries around the country, culminating in the full blown and extended miners' strike.

Suddenly I found that I had a new divisional responsibility! The Home Office had quickly realised that the Northern Forces could not sustain the demands on their numbers necessary to retain control of militant miners' picket lines. Disorder at various collieries was becoming the norm. To maintain peaceful and lawful picketing, police forces around the country were being required to supply large numbers of police support units (PSUs) to police forces in Yorkshire, Sheffield and Derbyshire. A PSU comprised of an inspector, two sergeants and 20 constables. Our division, was being required to supply a minimum of three PSUs a week! Three inspectors, six sergeants and 60 constables removed from the division's operational strength every week took a lot of managing, and the task often fell to me. It could only be done by cancelling all unnecessary leave and by offering the commitment as overtime. The posting was always difficult and quite stressful duty – the men (it was mainly men) received a lot of verbal and sometimes physical abuse. The accommodation, usually rundown and abandoned ex-military camps, were often barely habitable. Food varied in quality although it was usually wholesome.

Nevertheless, the hours spent on the deployment, all at overtime rates, attracted much larger pay packets to the men involved and very soon I found that I was having to manage from another perspective!

Initially I had struggled to find volunteers, now I was having to ensure that the opportunity to earn more money was shared out equitably.

Later it was realised that with the force sending out so many PSUs each month – sometimes 10 to 12 PSU units at a time – there was now an additional need to send Superintendents as local commanders and also Chief Inspectors as liaison officers. On one occasion I was deployed to the Sheffield and Derbyshire area, mainly in order to gain experience for what was expected to become a very extended commitment. I travelled up to Sheffield with one of the three PSUs supplied by my St George station. The inspector in charge of the serial was Brian Roebuck, the stern traditional disciplinarian.

Our responsibility was night cover at three Derbyshire pits. We were actually billeted at RAF Bawtry, a camp now de-militarised and almost derelict. The accommodation comprised of a number of wooden Nissan type huts with 20 bunks in each hut. The inspector had a small separate area at the end of the hut. I was accommodated in a smaller hut which I shared with the superintendent from our force in local control. There were no curtains at the windows but to enable sleep to take place during the day, newspaper was stuck to the windows. It was not five-star living!

We worked a 12-hour shift from 8 pm until 8 am, one PSU at each mine with others in reserve. My role was to maintain a mobile supervisory brief on all three pits. Brian Roebuck kept a very strong grip on his men and I noticed him putting them through extra drill practice on more than one occasion. His PSU was always smarter than the others, although they were not necessarily the happiest.

On our final night's duty we returned to Bawtry just after 8 am and immediately bedded down to prepare for our trip back down south and home. Without warning, the door of our hut smashed open and I saw in the doorway an enraged Brian Roebuck. He was giving a very good impression of the Incredible Hulk and I would not have been surprised to have seen his shirt splitting at the seams. Supt Rigg and myself managed to calm him down a little and I went with him back to his hut to examine the cause of his anger.

I didn't have to look far. His bunk and the whole floor of his billet was crawling with bright red fishing maggots! Someone had seemed to think it a good idea to acquire a large flagon of these fishing maggots and empty them into his bed. I would have been upset too!

Obviously this could not be tolerated and Supt Rigg and I immediately commenced an investigation. Supt Rigg interviewed all the sergeants and constables in the hut, and I went into Bawtry to locate the source of the infestation. That didn't take too long as there was a fishing tackle shop not far away in the village. Yes, they had sold a pint of maggots earlier that morning but no they couldn't remember who had bought them, indeed they really didn't want to help at all. They had clearly been briefed to say nothing!

The actual culprit was never identified, however the actions of a small group of troublemakers had brought discredit on our force, and a very severe indication of my disgust was required. They were left in no doubt that this was a very serious breach of what I expected of them, and that as a result none of them would be selected for this sort of duty for a very long time. This was going to cost each and every one of them a great deal in lost overtime.

As the year wore on, the manpower demands of the miners' strike gradually reduced and normal policing resumed. Then in about early November I was advised that I had been allocated a place on the important 'Junior Command Course' at the Police Staff College at Bramshill House, near Basingstoke, Hampshire. The course was of six months' duration, commencing at the start of January 1984.

The course, which I later assessed as a three-month course which had been squeezed into six months, was based on perceived advanced strategic thinking, making use of lectures and visits to significant industrial complexes etc. There were also a number of workshops involving tribunals and evolving employment law, etc.

One aspect of the course was a requirement whilst at the college to complete a 9,000-word thesis on a police-related subject. The importance of this element of the course was underlined by the fact that the eventual assessment of the completed thesis would not only form part of our final course report, but would also be sent to our chief constable. With that in mind, it was clearly essential that the document should be relevant and interesting.

I looked at the suggested subjects and could find nothing that inspired me with any enthusiasm. Then my mind went back to my days planning royal visits etc. and my travels in HM's helicopters. I realised that the overview obtained from an aircraft flying at about 500 feet was remarkable, and if properly dedicated to police use, an aircraft would provide a significant aid to command and control of any incident on the ground. Yes! This would be subject of my thesis. Apart from anything else, the concept of aerial policing was very new, so the possibility of my thesis being shot down by some expert at the college was minimal. With decision, police air support was to become my concentrated effort for the next few months, and although I didn't know it then, was to feature very much in my life for the next three decades!

The Metropolitan Police had purchased three big Bell 206, twin-engined helicopters for use over London. At about the same time, in the far west of the country, Devon and Cornwall police were experimenting with a single-engined French Squirrel helicopter. Hampshire were experimenting with using a fixed-wing Cessna aircraft for police air observations and were also looking at the new Edgley Optica aircraft. There was a great deal of research to be done.

I arranged a number of visits to the Metropolitan Police at their new air support unit at Lippetts Hill in Epping Forest. During my time with them they were good enough to fly me on several missions over central London, and from that practical experience I became more and more convinced of the potential for using aircraft in the search for missing persons and persons responsible for street crime.

My research also required visits to the Devon and Cornwall police air support unit at Middlemoor, Exeter, and to the small fixed-wing unit operating from Lee on Solent airfield, near Gosport in Hampshire.

By the end of the JCC in June 1984, I had completed my thesis on 'The use of Aircraft in Police Operations' and I had recommended that we looked seriously at acquiring a single-engined fixed-wing aircraft to assist with searches for missing persons and suspect vehicles. It was submitted to my force in the normal way but received little support from the senior officers that read it. Indeed, I was forced to conclude that the only person that I had convinced at the time was me!

My general end-of-course report was very good indeed, and so my unimpressive thesis was not later to become a burden to me. However it had lit a very strong conviction in my mind that there was a need to make use of the unique advantage that an aerial platform could provide. I had clearly missed something. What was it?

Then light dawned! I had become swayed by the desire to introduce a cheap facility to the service and had fallen into the trap of not properly defining the actual need. In following the cheapest possible solution I had arrived at an almost First World War idea of aerial observation. Then observation 'scout' aeroplanes had flown over enemy lines and perhaps taken pictures, but had no method of reporting what they had seen until they had flown back to their own lines.

My thesis concept had not been much different. The fixed-wing observation aircraft I had suggested had no direct communication with police officers on the ground, and it could not land and intervene in any incident. Its effectiveness was therefore very limited.

On reflection later, it was of no surprise that my report had fallen on deaf ears. There had to be a better way, and I was not going to give up!

Back at St George I threw myself back into my deputy sub-divisional commander role of supporting Roy Jones.

He was proving to be a great boss, and I was enjoying learning from his calm and knowledgable persona almost daily.

One day we received notification of a major anti-drugs raid that was being planned to take place at a well-known cafe in St Pauls. The area had been the scene of a major riot in 1980 and so it was anticipated that trouble would also follow this operation. However, this time we were to be better prepared than we were in 1980. Now all police officers were equipped with flame retardant uniforms, and were regularly trained in the use of riot shields and public disorder control tactics.

Our division, like all the other Bristol divisions, was required to supply four police support units, our contribution was two units. I would travel with them in support of Superintendent Robin Jones who would command a sector on the ground. The Southmead sub division had also supplied Chief Inspector David Rigg and the two of us would work closely with Robin Jones.

The raid went off as planned and initially things remained fairly quiet but then just as the incident control started to withdraw officers from the most central area, disorder started to break out. Bricks were being thrown and the occasional petrol bomb.

David Rigg and myself were speaking with Robin Jones near a block of flats. He was briefing us about what he wanted us to do. I suddenly noticed that his eyes had crossed, and he collapsed soundlessly to the ground. He had been hit on the back of the head by a missile. I remember David and myself immediately trying to establish which one of us was senior in rank and should take over! It was David, but we actually had little choice in what happened next, we had to withdraw.

Robin Jones, although having been knocked out by the thrown missile, made a full recovery after spending a few hours in hospital.

Our transit vans were hailed and we were getting everyone together ensuring that we had accounted for everyone. Suddenly, one of my youngest officers was engulfed in flames as a petrol bomb smashed at the foot of his shield. Luckily our new equipment proved its worth and, apart from some singed eyebrows, he came through it unscathed, if a little shocked.

Actually I took the slightly more painful injuries. I learned quickly that you could see the firebombs coming quite easily, but the most dangerous things looked like black dots arching over towards us.

Those black dots were bricks. I took two in quick succession!

The standard police riot shield, often carried in public order situations by constables and sergeants, is a full-length carbon plastic shield, designed to protect the full length of the officer from thrown missiles. The full-length shield is, however, quite cumbersome and tends to restrict the ability to move quickly. So in order to provide greater flexibility of movement required by officers in command of such situations, senior officers carried small shields. Sadly, these short shields did not offer the same level of protection as the normal full-length ones.

The first brick grazed down the right side of my face and bounced painfully off my shoulder. The second was the most painful, coming in under my shield and impacting on my left knee. That one hurt a great deal more, but in the excitement of the situation the adrenaline was pulsing and I didn't really feel much pain until the situation had calmed down.

We got the PSUs safely away but none of the officers from our sector were happy with the critical lack of communication during that operation. It was quite wrong to withdraw large numbers of officers from the front line without telling us what they were doing. That failure to communicate had put us in a very vulnerable position and I made a point of saying so. We returned to St George to lick our wounds.

Luckily the situation did not escalate and we were able to stand down after a couple of days.

There was no doubt by now that St George Police Station had seen better days and it was starting to get noticed. Suddenly the local evening paper, the Evening Post, ran a big centre spread article with photograph, asking the question "Is this Britain's Worst Police Station? Built in 1861, and not a penny spent on it ever since!" It was a really scathing article.

Very soon after its publication, Roy Jones called me into his office and told me that the next day we were going to be visited and inspected by the Police Authority. He indicated that he would show them around, but wanted me outside the station on the opposite side of the road when their bus came up the hill from Bristol, in order to greet them and see them safely over the road and into the station. Simple! Well at least in theory.

The next day at the appointed time I was waiting as directed on the opposite side of the road, and spotted the bus coming towards me.

The bus stopped where directed and I gathered the 17 members of the Police Authority together and asked them to wait whilst I stopped the busy traffic for them.

I stepped out into the middle of the road and faced down the incline in the direction of Bristol. I gave a very smart number one stop signal and all the traffic came gracefully to a halt! Then I did a smart about-turn, facing up the hill in the direction of Kingswood. There were several cars coming down the hill and so I pointed clearly to a car about 20 yards away that I wanted to stop, threw up a number one stop signal and expected a smooth stopping of the traffic. No! The car closest to me slammed on his brakes and I heard a loud squealing of several other lots of brakes and then crash! A car had slammed into the back of the third car in the queue. Then there was a sort of tinkling noise as a hub cap rolled down the road.

This somewhat embarrassed and red-faced chief inspector ushered the members of the Police Authority across the road. But the very last one to cross, a lady, grinned at me and said, "Very good chief inspector, what are you going to do for an encore?"

You know we often speak about poor communication, but within 15 minutes of that happening, I received a telephone call from a friend in Yeovil asking if I was having a bad day! My embarrassment was complete.

As deputy sub-divisional commander at St George I was expected to perform duty as acting superintendent whenever my boss Supt Roy Jones was absent for more than just a few days. But by 1986, Roy's absence was becoming more frequent and it was obvious that he was looking forward to his retirement. I was more than happy to stand in, and was very happy with the 'acting' pay that I received as a result.

Like all periods of 'acting' at a superior rank in the police service, the first 14 days in any year, starting on the 1st April each year, was regarded as valuable experience and not rewarded by any increase in pay. Then after that first 14 days in the higher rank, you were paid a daily rate commensurate with the first year of service in the higher rank.

Superintendents were under a totally different pay structure to that which applied to the 'federated ranks' i.e. from constable to chief inspector who were all in receipt of overtime pay when overtime was worked. Superintendents and chief superintendents were members of a different pay structure negotiated by the superintendents' association and effectively were salaried. In other words, they were paid to do their job however long it took, and were not able to claim overtime for any extra time worked. The superintendents' pay scale was significantly higher than that received by chief inspectors, in recognition of their 24-hour responsibility and their inability to claim overtime. This significant difference was soon to work against me on one particular occasion!

Later that year I was performing duty as acting superintendent at St George when one evening a significant riot broke out in Horfield Prison, Bristol. The prison was located right on our border with Bristol, and as it was also my night as divisional duty officer I became responsible for preparing the divisional response to increasing requests for task forces and PSUs to be sent to the prison. Our response from St George was a PSU led by the indomitable Inspector Brian Roebuck.

The prisoners had taken over several blocks in the prison and several fires had broken out. It was obvious that significant damage was being done and prison staff were in danger. Our PSUs forced entry to the prison, assisted by a team of specialist prison officers who had now arrived from other prisons in England.

The riot was subdued with some difficulty in the middle of the night and I was constantly updating Silver Control with the current situation. It was late in the morning of the following day before I could retire home for some sleep. By then I had been on constant duty for about 27 hours.

It had been a very interesting night and I had gained a lot of new experience, but I quickly realised that for me it was a non-earner.

I was officially rostered as the acting superintendent and so even though my substantive rank was that of chief inspector, as an acting superintendent I was prevented from claiming any overtime pay. But to make matters even worse, I was still within my first 14 'free' days in the higher rank so I wouldn't even be paid any 'acting money'.

I am told my friends say that they heard me muttering fiercely, "I guess I shouldn't have joined if I couldn't take a joke!" Ah well!

The same year it also became evident that the visit of inspection by the Police Authority had paid dividends, and it was announced that St George would be closed temporarily and we would run the sub division from the much smaller Lockleaze station. St George would be completely modernised internally and would be closed for at least 18 months.

Superintendent Roy Jones then announced his retirement and I continued in an acting capacity until a new substantive Superintendent David Parkin was appointed in early 1987.

David Parkin was totally different to Roy Jones in character, and was clearly a different but just as effective leader. He had a strong North Yorkshire accent, was much younger than Roy and very fit. His lunchtimes were spent running around several local parks instead of playing snooker. He was always keen to engage with his staff, both serving and civilian, and took an active interest in their welfare.

On the social and domestic side, my life was changing too. The small three-bedroom house we had bought in Longwell Green back in 1979 had already become very cramped. Our three children were growing up quickly and the two girls were having to share a bedroom. So in 1985 we had moved to a much larger detached four-bedroom house in Stoke Gifford.

By 1982 I had realised that in a few years time I would be 40, and as a result would have to leave Round Table which had an upper age limit of 40 years. You were then expected to leave and perhaps join some other similar organisation. I was still very grateful to Rotary International who had earlier sent me on the exchange visit to Japan.

The problem for me was that in the early 80s most Rotary Clubs still held weekly meetings at a lunchtime venue. This clearly did not fit comfortably with my life as a police officer. However, I discovered that in other areas of the United Kingdom, a number of evening clubs had opened which were more suited to modern commercial pressures. This new style of Rotary Club was exactly what I wanted, and through contacts that I had maintained after Japan, I commenced the creation of a new evening club based on the outer fringe of northeast Bristol. We called it Bristol East Avon Rotary Club. We cheated a little on the requirement to meet weekly by deciding to have full meetings with a meal and speaker only on the first and third Tuesday of the month and on the second and fourth Tuesday we would have short half hour meetings to discuss club business. It worked well and soon we had 30 members and a great social life together.

Membership of Rotary International was soon to bring about another adventure for me. Many years previously Rotary had created its 'Foundation', an international charity dedicated to advancing world peace by fostering international fellowship and understanding. It was the Rotary Foundation that in 1981 had sent me on the group study exchange trip to Japan. I had joined Rotary in 1982 with the formation of my new club and by 1988 I had become the Rotary District Foundation Chairman, a post that I enjoyed very much.

In late 1988 I was approached by the then district governor of our Rotary District, Ken Broad (of cricketing family fame), and he asked me if I would like to be his representative on a new group study exchange trip to South Australia. The trip would be of six weeks duration and I would be the team leader of a new concept for the district as it was to be an all-female team!

Obviously the appointment was a great honour, but first I had to obtain permission from Paula, my long-suffering wife, and that of the chief constable and Police Authority. Luckily, all three agreed and so we set about interviewing applicants and appointing the team.

We selected Helen Rogers, a turbine blade engineer from Rolls Royce, Linda Duley, an agricultural botanist from Bromsgrove, Jean Jones a detective constable from Bristol, Julia Goss a bank employee from Leominster and Helena Cava a social worker from Clevedon. Each was outstanding in their field of expertise and would now be studying and working in that specialism in Australia.

We were due to leave for South Australia in March 1989 so I only had a few months to form them into a team. I initially worried that being such very different characters they would fight, but I was very wrong in that assumption. They gelled immediately and were soon working very well together. They recognised the fact that they were representing the very best from our region of England, and understood the importance of getting their presentations perfect.

I was immensely proud of my team, and realised from very early on that this was going to be an outstanding trip.

Kangaroo | © Kangaroo Island Seasons

13

An Antipodean Interlude!

The team flew out of Heathrow in early March 1989, arriving in Adelaide about 24 hours later. Quantas had been a great airline to fly with and understanding that we were effectively a national team, arranged for us to have changing facilities on board. That meant that we could fly comfortably, but then change in order to arrive at our destination wearing smart uniform.

We were met at the airport by senior Rotarians from District 950 Australia, including Brian Burt the team leader for the team that would be visiting the UK. Then each of the team was introduced to their host family for a couple of days of very necessary acclimatisation. There had been snow on the ground in England when we left but now in South Australia, even though the really hot summer was over for them, the local temperature was in the 80 degrees Fahrenheit.

We were all staying with families in West Lakes, a fairly new and very nice development just outside Adelaide itself. All of the houses were either large bungalows or chalet-style houses. All had very nice swimming pools!

By now I had received a final and detailed itinerary and that confirmed that our first real test was to attend the Rotary District's annual conference on Kangaroo Island which was located just off the coast of South Australia. The island had a total population of about 800 people, but the conference would almost double that number over the three main days that it was held. What did worry me a little was that my programme said quite clearly that we would be crossing to the island with the 'Philanderer'. That sounded a bit dodgy to me. I was responsible for the girls and I knew that Aussies could be a bit full on occasionally so travelling anywhere with a Philanderer was going to be a bit risky.

At the end of the acclimatisation period, the team met up again and we all set off on a coach to Victor Harbour where we were to board a large boat heading to Kingscote on Kangaroo Island. I was more than a little relieved to see the name on the stern of the boat. It was The Philandera!

We arrived on K.I. (as everyone called it) in the late afternoon and it was quite clear that a large party was just about starting. There was good country-style music being played. Everyone was seated around a makeshift dance floor, on hay bales or logs, and there was a great deal of beer and wine in evidence. I discovered later that the local police officer had had an accident with his breathalyser kit and had dropped it causing it to break. That was a bit of a shame, however he did not appear too concerned stating that his sergeant would understand.

I later discovered that he was by coincidence a member of the local Rotary Club.

As the evening wore on, one by one the girls were claimed by their Rotary host families and driven off into the night. Being the ugly one, I was last to be claimed. Ray Kingham was the president of the Rotary Club of Kangaroo Island, and with his wife Barbara was to host me for the five days that the team would spend on the island. The three of us jumped into his battered Toyota Landcruiser and headed off down dirt roads for what seemed like an hour, until we arrived at their farmstead near Parndana in the centre of the island.

It was dark when we arrived but I saw enough to realise that although the farmstead was quite large it was comparatively basic compared to the luxury we had experienced when we had first arrived in West Lakes – it had a corrugated tin roof!

We were up early the next morning, the morning of the conference. But Ray and Barbara needed to feed their cattle first. They had an old 'Yute', the Aussie term for a utility truck or type of jeep. It was loaded with hay bales. Ray drove across some open paddocks until we came to a small herd of beef cattle sheltering under some trees which provided some shade from the already hot sun. Barbara was clearly the strong one of the two, and stood up in the back of the Yute, hurling hay bales out at the cattle trotting behind. She surely was a formidable woman and she reminded me very much of the actress Peggy Mount!

That job done we changed back to the Landcruiser and headed for Kingscote and the conference.

By the time I arrived in Parndana the rest of the team had already arrived and were clustered together in a small group obviously swapping notes about their experiences with this new set of host families. Generally they were all quite happy and looking forward to their contribution to the conference. However, I noticed that Julia was not smiling at all and indeed looked quite close to tears. I went over and took her to one side. She immediately said, "Brian, I'm not sure if I'm going to be able to hack this!" I expressed surprise recalling that she had earlier expressed an interest in the Guiding fraternity. She said, "I was quite scared last night, my host had obviously had a few drinks and his driving was a bit erratic!" I said, "Oh well, it was quite a party, but you were obviously OK because you're here now!" She said, "That wasn't the problem, the house had a tin roof and was pretty basic, they showed me to my room and there weren't any curtains at the windows."

I said, "Never mind, there probably wasn't anyone outside for miles and miles!" She said, "That wasn't the problem either, I wanted to go to the toilet, they showed me a little wooden hut outside, they called it the dunny, and there were two fierce dogs between me and it!"

I remember thinking then, this was certainly going to be an experience!

In the event, the conference went very well indeed and the whole team were superb. They quickly got used to their host families and learned to appreciate that life on K.I. was very different to life in the state capital Adelaide. Kangaroo Island had been given its name by the English navigator and cartographer, Captain Mathew Flinders who, on his ship HMS Investigator, first charted the territory then entitled 'New Holland'. Flinders actually discovered it to be a whole new continent and named it Terra Australis, later Australia. It was whilst exploring around the southern coast of the new continent that Flinders and his crew, desperately short of food and fresh water, landed on the island and found it to be abundant in the required supplies. The meat, of course, in the form of an abundance of medium-sized brown kangaroos. The name was never changed.

We were scheduled to spend a full week on the island and that gave our host families a great opportunity to show us around. The Flinders Chase national park was literally full of brown kangaroos.

The brown is a breed specific to the island and are a little smaller than the mainland red and grey varieties. What amused me were several large cages made of tall steel bars where the tourists could watch the kangaroos and eat their picnics safe from the attention of the hungry roos. The difference of course being that the tourists were the ones in the cages and the animals were the ones freely hopping about on the outside! Each cage had a door with a secure latch, together with picnic tables and chairs. You would drive up, unpack the picnic before the animals realised what was happening, lock yourself in the cage and enjoy your food whilst the animals watched you through the bars.

We loved it. The whole island was full of exotic wildlife. On Ray and Barb's farmstead there were koalas in the tree tops, emus in the paddocks and Cape Barren geese wandering about too. We visited Remarkable Rocks on the southwestern end of the island which had an incredible rock formation, some of them seemingly balanced at quite strange angles. The shores of the island were covered in a local sea lion population and large flocks of pelicans were actively fishing by diving into the sea at high speed. The whole island seemed to be in effect a living zoo.

The only negative at all was that bathing was impossible in all but the shallowest of waters because the seas around South Australia were the home of the great white shark! We were also warned to be careful near water courses as they attracted the king brown snake, one of the most venomous in Australia.

On our last full day on K.I., Ray and Barb announced that they were holding a BBQ for the team and some other host friends. However, I could tell that Ray was a bit worried about something. Then suddenly he spotted a dust cloud getting closer coming along the dirt road, and he looked much happier. It was his delivery of several months' supply of port. It was delivered in an old battered Yute, the whole back of which was full of large plastic flagons, each filled with port. I hadn't realised until then, but port was very popular in South Australia.

It was a very good BBQ, and the team were quite sad to be leaving K.I. the next day.

The organising Rotary District had chartered a twin-engined Cessna aircraft to take us from Kangaroo Island to our next stop which was the very beautiful coastal town of Port Lincoln, several hundred miles west of Adelaide around the Spencer Gulf.

Port Lincoln was another incredibly beautiful location. The small town had a large marina, home to hundreds of fishing boats, some quite small but others large and powerful. They were mainly working boats for this was a tuna-catching region. Indeed, tuna fishing was the main commercial industry of the community. Nearly every family owned their own boat and would be out most days catching tuna by rod and line. Every boat was surmounted by two huge rods in a V formation when viewed from ahead or astern. These huge rods trailed lines ending in large and very sharp hooks. Tuna caught in this way were then processed in one of several large community canneries and then shipped all over the world. It was big business for Port Lincoln.

There was also a second and rapidly growing seafood industry in Port Lincoln, that of farming huge crayfish. These 'crays' were farmed in very large submerged pens out in the clear blue waters of the bay. When they got to the size of a large lobster, they would be collected from the pens, placed in a large water-filled plastic bag, oxygen would be pumped in and the bag sealed. Within a few hours the still live crays would be on their way to Japan by plane, where each one would fetch several hundred Australian dollars in a city restaurant.

Port Lincoln was clearly a very successful and thriving community. It even had its own very well-supported horse racing track, stud farm and stabling facilities.

My host Bruce Bennett was the president of Port Lincoln Rotary Club and he and his wife Irene ran a hotel and sport fishing business. His powerful sport fishing boat was fitted with two huge diesel engines, capable of pushing the boat to high speed. He insisted on taking us all out fishing one day and we caught a number of fish for the BBQ that night. He offered to lower anyone over the side in a shark-proof cage if we wanted to see a great white close up, but sadly there were no takers for that treat!

Soon we were on the road again, this time in two small buses on the main highway around the Spencer Gulf, in the direction of a very distant Adelaide.

Our first scheduled stop was in Whyalla, a smaller and much quieter town than Port Lincoln. Whyalla had suffered badly in the recent downturn in the Australian economy. It was once a centre for ship building and other heavy industries, but sadly these were now all closed. Once again the team were all billeted with local rotarians. We were made to feel extremely welcome and our hosts took great delight in taking us to their golf club in the evening. I do enjoy golf but this was very different. The holes were surrounded by smooth burnt earth and the fairways were of a much rougher scrub. The real problem was a mob of big grey kangaroos who were lying about all over the place, idly scratching and throwing dirt on themselves.

The most memorable thing for me was the town's war memorial. Like nearly all Australian war memorials, this was not a stone cenotaph or cross, but something that was a stark reminder of the war. I had previously experienced army tanks or a field gun, or perhaps an aircraft, but bearing in mind Whyalla's past history of ship building their war memorial was a complete Flower Class Corvette, HMAS Whyalla!

She had been built in Whyalla in 1940 and had served her time with the Royal Australian Navy. But in 1950, when she was no longer required and was due to be scrapped, she was pulled out of the water, surrounded by a supporting cradle and turned into Whyalla's war memorial. She is still there today in 2019.

Then we moved further east to Port Augusta. This community had once been an important mining and industrial centre and as a result appeared to be covered in an orange-brown dust, probably a residue from earlier days when its port was the export route for copper ore mined and smelted in the Flinders ranges. The town had survived the depression of the eighties, was now recovering, becoming a minor regional centre for several companies. Importantly it was also a regional centre for the Flying Doctor service, which I was pleased to visit. As the visit progressed, they quickly recognised my aviation interests and offered me a ride along on one of their regular Flying GP services.

The flight was a fascinating experience. We took off from Port Augusta airfield in a twin-engined Cessna aircraft and flew on a huge circular clockwise circuit of several hundreds of miles. We landed at a number of outback airfields serving small communities and set up a surgery from the back of the aircraft. The people knew that the aircraft would visit every other Tuesday afternoon for example. And so if they needed to see a doctor in a non-emergency situation, they would wait for the regular visit. Emergencies were of course very different and then a radio call would be made to summons the emergency flying doctor on call.

Outback landings were always fun. Just imagine the scene! As we arrive overhead the outback landing strip, you could see the airstrip easily. On either side of the strip would be a wide cleared area, so that the wings of the aircraft would not come into contact with any obstructions. It's early afternoon and it is very hot. Either side of the strip lying in the sun are a number of big grey kangaroos. They are half asleep, and have covered themselves in dust as protection. A big male grey is woken from his slumbers by the sound of the aircraft, and remembers that lovely young female kangaroo he saw on the other side of the strip just before he got tired. Perhaps now would be a good time to visit her. Not for us it isn't!

So the standard procedure was to keep the wheels tucked up in the belly of the aircraft and fly as fast as we could at very low level down the length of the runway, making as much noise as possible. We would do that several times until the pilot was happy that all the animals had hopped off away from the strip and we could make a safe landing.

Port Augusta was also the base from which we were scheduled to go on a four-day 'outback safari' led by Malcolm Butler. Malcolm owned a small but highly recommended outback safari company. His family had lived in the area for many many years, and I suspect that there was not a lot that Malcolm did not know about the outback. We would be travelling in two highly modified Toyota Landruisers, both towing military style trailers loaded with extra fuel, tents, water and food. Malcolm would drive one and his friend Bernie Swan the other. His daughter Helen came along too to help with the cooking. I knew instinctively that the six members of our team were in very safe hands.

We set off from Port Augusta heading north towards the Flinders Ranges. We stopped at Quorn for some supplies, and then continued along bitumen roads which soon turned to compressed dirt tracks. I noticed that the once clear blue skies had suddenly turned very threatening. There was a loud crack of thunder and torrential rain fell for most of the day. Dry creek beds filled rapidly with fast flowing water and the dirt tracks we were using quickly became a quagmire. The Toyotas were struggling to make headway. They would normally have been able to cope, being tough 4x4s built for this sort of treatment, but the heavy trailers we were towing made things very difficult for us. The girls were getting quite good at de-ditching the vehicles using stout spades. I watched things carefully to avoid accidents. It was obviously part of my team leader responsibilities to ensure that they were OK.

Eventually, Malcolm said we had done enough for the day and we stopped at a small outback settlement that had a sort of unstaffed road house where you could stop overnight and bed down. It was basic but dry and there were wooden bed frames to lay out our swag bags or tough sleeping bags. Once, in the middle of the night there was a squeal of consternation from the girls and I saw in the torchlight a green frog crawling up the walls in their room.

Next day we pressed on through ever tougher and more remote bush, the sun and heat were back and the going much better than in the mud the day before. Malcolm was clearly following a well-known path to him, but to us the route appeared totally random and devoid of an obvious track. But after a long day's travel we arrived at a derelict settlement long vacated by early settlers. Here at 'Sliding Rock' we would spend another night before finally making it to our planned destination of Wilpena Pound, up in the Flinders Ranges.

Each night we set up camp around the camp fire on which Malcolm had prepared coffee and good camp food. The girls were each supplied with single tents but very quickly found that they were magnets for flies and creepy crawlies, and so soon joined Malcolm, Bruce and I on their swag bags around the fire.

The safari was certainly toughening up the team! As I saw Julia wondering off into the bush the next morning carrying a spade, my mind went back to that first morning on Kangaroo Island when she had been worried about the dunny!

Despite the remoteness of where we were, Malcom was able to show us all sorts of flora and fauna that we had never seen before. The heavy rain of two days previously, although now only a distant memory, was turning the outback into flashes of beautiful colour. Yellow desert lilies were springing up all around and also pink Easter lilies. The national flower of South Australia, Sturts desert pea, is a beautiful red flower with a jet black eye. The flower extended just a few inches in height from a network of tendrils growing in the sand of the bush. (Col Charles Sturt had been a famous early explorer of the outback.) That part of the Flinders was covered in the salt bushes which gave the 'bush' its name. Everywhere there were green and yellow budgerigars, pink and grey galahs and white cockatoos flying about in large noisy flocks.

One day I nearly stood on a large fat and very aggressive lizard. Malcolm said it was a blue tongued or stumpy lizard. Not poisonous but as Malcolm said, you don't want to get bitten by one as they don't brush their teeth very often and the wound can get infected. That reminded him to warn us that if we 'put up' (scared) an iguana and it was running towards us, we had to throw ourselves on the ground. That sounded wrong to me and I questioned the wisdom of throwing myself on the ground in front of a three-foot long lizard. Malcolm's reply was, "Yes, he's scared, he's got very poor eyesight so his best form of defence is to run up the tallest thing around and look about to see what had scared him, and what's more he has got very sharp claws. You don't want him running up you!"

All too soon our wonderful outback safari was over and the team was headed for our next stop, the small town of Peterborough. Once again, this was to be a very different and thought-provoking experience for all of us. It transpired that Peterborough was an almost exclusively Lutheran community that had moved en masse from Bavarian Germany to South Australia just over 100 years ago.

They built up the community township of Petersburg and had lived a happy existence there ever since. However, after the First World War, when so many young Australians and New Zealanders had been killed fighting in Europe, it was felt that advertising their Germanic background by calling their town Petersburg was not a good idea.

So Petersburg had become Peterborough!

My host family were the Van Brussels. Father Peter, mother and three children. They lived a frugal and very religious existence. At each mealtime we all ate together seated around a round table. Each person had to read a verse from the Bible in turn, including me, and each morning we attended a local chapel for a short service.

Although being a Christian by faith, I cannot claim to be a regular churchgoer but I have to say that the few days that I spent in that community with the Van Brussel family were some of the most peaceful and wonderful days I have ever had.

Peterborough had another and very memorable claim to fame in that it was once one of the major rail centres in the whole of Australia. It possessed a very strangely sounding 'bogie exchange'. It was necessary because the five huge states that formed the continent of Australia had each developed at different times and speeds and very often chose different railway gauges to their neighbours. But as the 20th century wore on and people wanted to criss cross the continent by rail, the differing gauges became a problem. Peterborough happened to be roughly in the centre of much of this activity and the authorities worked out a very important solution to the problem. The bogie exchange!

A carriage fitted with bogies from its state of origin would be shunted under a lifting crane, which then lifted the entire carriage into the air. The two sets of bogies would then be removed and replaced by others suited to the gauge used by the destination state. Passengers would have to get out, of course, but all their baggage could remain on board whilst this was happening. As a result of this invention, Peterborough soon became a major rail centre in Australia.

Sadly, after the Second World War came the dawn of civil aviation and flying became the main answer to covering the huge distances across Australia. Peterborough became almost a ghost town.

But there in the centre of the town we found a huge wooden roundhouse filled with rusting and derelict steam engines and carriages. It was so sad. However, the worm of history was once again turning. By 1989, nostalgia was awakening an interest in restoring some of the old engines and the track stretching out over miles of flat bush. Steam train rides were on offer and the team enjoyed a day out and a trackside picnic.

I am told that today the revival continues and that there is now a thriving railway museum centred on Peterborough. Oh how I would love to see that again.

Our trip was coming to its final few weeks and it was time for each member to spend some time in and around Adelaide working in their own occupational interest. A great deal of effort had been put into selecting the most appropriate attachments for all of the team, including myself. I was to be attached to the South Australian Police Air Wing.

The only issue that had threatened to mar the whole of the trip for me had been the unfortunate attitude of the organising Rotary District towards my wife Paula. The team visiting England from South Australia had come to England in the previous autumn and like mine was an all -female team, except of course its leader Brian Burt. Brian was accompanied by his wife Ann and Paula and I had spent a lot of time with them and ensured that their team had a good time.

I had naturally assumed that when the time came for me to lead our team on the return visit, that Paula would accompany me on the trip. However, we suddenly received a communication from the South Australian District in about January 1989, that they had been unaware that Ann had accompanied their team on the trip to England, Brian had been reprimanded and that Paula's inclusion on our visit was not agreed.

It was too late by that stage for me to stand down but I did write a strongly worded letter of protest citing that I was aware that on previous exchanges involving female teams that team leaders had been accompanied by wives as chaperones at their own expense.

The letter I received in response only served to increase my anger in that they reluctantly accepted that Paula could accompany me on the visit, but that we were both required to sign a declaration that "Her presence in Australia would not adversely affect the performance of the team." This was nothing short of an insult!

Paula was understandably dreadfully upset and immediately declared that there was no way that she would now come to Australia with me. The matter was closed but it had left a nasty taste. However that was not to be the end of it!

Two weeks later we received a private letter from Brian Burt explaining that the whole unfortunate episode had been an overreaction by District 950 to a disastrous exchange visit the previous year.

An Antipodean Interlude! **159**

That particular visit, which had not involved a team from the UK, had been marred by poor behaviour and as a result had greatly embarrassed the organising clubs. On hearing of Paula's distress, Brian's Club, Gawler Rotary Club, and two other clubs near Adelaide, had immediately acted to privately invite Paula to stay with them during the final two weeks of the exchange, whilst my team would be in their area during the vocational element of the tour. This kind offer was gratefully accepted and as a result Paula flew out to Australia for the final two weeks of the exchange visit. She flew alone on her first ever flight in an aircraft. I was very proud of her.

However, these arrangements were unofficial and as a result we had all agreed not to impart this little gem to the receiving district organisers. I therefore had the amusing task of arranging several clandestine meetings with my own wife during that period. In the end, the district organisers realised their overreaction to the previous team's behaviour, apologised for their misjudgement and happily involved Paula and the whole team in the final celebrations.

My attachment to the South Australia Police Air Wing was very interesting indeed. However, it was very different to the concept that I was following for operations in the UK. Our crime rate was a much more serious problem than in Australia. As a result, our priority was to fight crime, especially vehicular crime, also to aid in searching for missing people. Their priority was almost exclusively distance related, in order to facilitate contact with officers posted hundreds of miles from their colleagues. Crime was a low priority in comparison. The air wing had three Cessna 403 twin-engined fixed-wing aircraft, two of which were in almost constant use. Mainly transporting officers in for court appearances, conveying deceased persons for the coroner's officer and also for spotting cannabis plantations. The drug problem was starting to cause some problems and once again distance was a factor. The drug dealers were establishing huge cannabis plantations hundreds of miles out in the bush. The air unit would make regular searches for them and, once discovered, a unit would be dispatched by road to set the plantation on fire. It was very rarely the culprits would be caught but at least their crops were burnt.

We returned to the UK in late April and I soon found myself reporting back for work at Lockleaze. St George had still not re opened.

Within a short time I was again summoned to HQ to see the Chief Constable David Shattock. He had once been our deputy chief constable, but a few years previously had moved to Dyfed Powys on promotion to be their chief. He had now returned to us as our chief. He informed me that he was moving me to become the sub-divisional commander at Filton. Filton was one of a small number of sub divisions within the force that were commanded by chief inspectors. They were regarded as excellent proving grounds for future success, and I was very pleased indeed to be given the opportunity.

Filton Police Station

14

Sub-Divisional Command

My appointment as sub-divisional commander at Filton was a new but very enjoyable experience for me. Firstly, for the first time since being the sergeant at Wincanton, I actually lived on the patch. Our move a few years earlier from our first small house in Longwell Green, to a bigger one in Stoke Gifford, meant that I actually lived right in the centre of Filton Sub Division.

The sub division had a great team of inspectors, sergeants and constables and they were all clearly well versed in what was required of them. The sub division was busy at all times and the crime rate and detection rate were acceptable. However, on studying all of the issues carefully I recognised immediately that the potential for disaster was greater at Filton than anywhere that I had ever served before.

British Aerospace, a major aircraft manufacturer, was based at Filton Airfield. In addition, American F111 fighter bombers were being maintained in the huge hangars located there, and were being test flown from the airfield almost daily. Rolls Royce aero engines were also manufactured on another site beside the airfield. The M4 and M5 motorways crossed at a big interchange at Almondsbury within the sub division, and the M32 motorway into Bristol centre also passed through.

Parkway Railway Station was Bristol's second biggest railway station and was a major station on the main line between Paddington Station in London and Swansea Station in Wales. The railway line passed under the Bristol Channel by way of the Severn Tunnel which had been dug under the seabed. The entrance to the Severn Tunnel was also on the sub-divisional 'at risk' list because the low lying land in that area also had a serious tendency to flood badly during certain combinations of high tides and adverse wind direction.

The sub division also boasted a nuclear power station which, although was due to be decommissioned in the near future, was still operational then. Yes, my Major Disaster disaster file was more than a little bulky and would require much careful study!

Finally, the sub division also hosted a major new 'out of town' shopping mall and entertainment complex at Cribbs Causeway, and one of Europe's biggest housing development areas at the new Bradley Stoke township where six or seven thousand homes were to be built.

This new responsibility was a little daunting, however previous experience gained throughout my career had given me the tools to deal with the challenges ahead. The most pressing of all the new responsibilities was the requirement to maintain a close liaison with BAE systems at Filton Airfield. Effectively that meant frequent contact with the airfield flight operations department. One of the issues was that the main A38 trunk road passed a matter of 50 yards from the end of the airfield's very long runway.

Discussions with flight ops soon brought me into close contact with two people who were to become key players in my desire to further develop the use of aircraft in the prevention and detection of crime. They were BAE Chief Test Pilot John Lewis, and the airfield's senior air traffic controller, Jeff Kellet. John was ex-RAF and a product of the internationally famous Empire Test Pilots School at Boscombe Down. Jeff was also ex-RAF, initially a navigator but later a highly experienced air traffic controller. Both of them went out of their way to assist me with general aviation advice and also, as the project made headway, by providing storage and accommodation for equipment gathered during extensive research.

By the late 1980s and also on into the 1990s, vehicular crime in the UK was reaching worrying proportions. Suddenly, stolen vehicles, very often 4x4s, were being reversed at high speed into shop fronts and through the shattered frontage cigarettes and alcohol were being stolen. The days of ram raiding had arrived. Dangerous high speed vehicle pursuits were happening in all our cities almost nightly. Yet there was very little the police could do to combat this new criminal activity. We had simply lost the initiative. The criminal realised that if they drove dangerously and at very high speed, the pursuing police officers would be instructed to cease the pursuit in the interest of public safety.

However, there was mounting evidence to show that in those areas where police forces had started to operate helicopters in support of their anti-crime operations, ram raiding and vehicle pursuits were far less of a problem. I redoubled my efforts to convince our force management team that we needed to look at this problem anew. It was an uphill struggle at first because all departments were increasing spending and budgets were very tight. However, by mid-1989 I had at least managed to get a subject line for air support on the force forward planning budget. I was also allocated a place on the Regional Air Support committee.

More importantly, the Home Office had also taken notice of the effectiveness of Police Air Support units in combatting crime. As a result, they were now encouraging more police forces to look at ways of availing themselves of this effective new resource.

In late spring 1989, the force was again preparing for the huge manpower commitment of the Pilton Pop Festival, or the Glastonbury music festival as it was now more commonly known. I proposed to Ch Superintendent Tug Wilson, my old boss at Support Services, that the pop festival would be an ideal time for me to be allowed to put into practice some of my ideas regarding airborne command and control. To my surprise he agreed and took my proposal to the ACC Operations, now Mike Hedges! He also supported, and as a result I was allowed to hire in a twin-engined Squirrel helicopter for five days. I had by that time already surrounded myself with a small but enthusiastic dedicated group of constables and sergeants as observers. We were ready to go. My two new contacts at BAE flight operations set aside a large room for me in their flight operations building free of any charge, and we set that up as our own dedicated flight operations centre for the pop festival.

The air support aspect of the operation went very well. We flew the chief constable and other senior officers over the site and by doing that we were able to bring a new aspect to the command and control of the event. In particular, the intelligence provided by our overview markedly improved traffic control around a wide area of southeast Somerset.

The force management team had expressed their appreciation of our efforts to enhance command and control over that particular event, but in reality the operation had disappointed me. I had realised very quickly that there were several key aspects regarding the use of aircraft that were preventing us from proving how effective air support could be in the fight against crime.

The most critical issue was our inability to talk to our police officers on the ground. In 1989, only those forces that had invested in the purchase of their own dedicated aircraft possessed the most rudimentary air-to-ground radio. My force was one of the vast majority of police forces that had not invested in air support, and therefore we had a very limited air support budget. As a result, it had only been on very rare occasions that we would hire in an aircraft from one of a very limited number of specialist helicopter operators. With such a small demand, they had not equipped any of their spare aircraft with even the most basic of police radio equipment.

With no effective air-to-ground communications, command and control of any major operation from the air could not be achieved. Until that hurdle could be overcome, police air operations could never really be successful. This was a major stumbling block and one that I realised we would have to overcome before we could really demonstrate how effective air support could be.

I resolved to keep up the pressure through membership of a number of advisory panels and committees in respect of police air support. The first thing that we needed to do was achieve a review of the allocation of radio band widths allocated to the police and emergency services. There had never previously been a frequency allocated for air-to-ground and vice versa communication, because there had been no demand for it. Rising crime, particularly vehicle-related crime, had changed the situation and demand was now rapidly increasing for dedicated air-to-ground frequencies both VHF and UHF. Put quite simply, police aircraft needed to be able to speak to individual officers on the ground. Only then would we really be able to provide proper support to them. It took a while but we finally achieved that vital change.

We also needed to modernise our onboard visual aids. We had started our earlier operations using ordinary binoculars, but these suffered greatly from the high frequency vibrations during helicopter flight. We soon adopted gyro-stabilised binoculars, but the problem was not really solved until the early 90s with the adoption of stabilised TV camera systems pioneered by the military and TV news-gathering aircraft. The development of these gyro-stabilised cameras progressed rapidly and within a very short time we were able to read a car number plate from over a half a mile away. The thermal imaging camera soon joined the TV camera in our all-seeing pod, so now the criminal could no longer rely on the cloak of darkness in which to carry out his activities.

The final major addition to our essential equipment was the adoption of GPS or global positioning systems. From the mid 90s, our 999 control rooms were able to include GPS coordinates of the source of the emergency. So our helicopter crews scrambling to get airborne to an emergency call could enter the map reference into the onboard computer and the aircraft would automatically plot the quickest route to the target.

In addition, our patrol cars would now carry their call signs painted on the roof so that we could identify and speak to a particular car.

But all of that was over and above my primary task of being the sub-divisional commander at Filton. My determination to pursue this new method of policing frequently brought negative comments from the chief officers who were facing significant cutbacks to policing budgets at the time. Indeed, on one occasion I received a written instruction from

Chief Constable David Shattock, I will always remember it, it read: "Much as I appreciate Chief Inspector Allinson's enthusiasm for the subject of Police Air Support, he must appreciate that there is no possibility of us being able to afford to do it. He really must desist!"

I noted the instruction and sadly must have misfiled it, because apparently it was never received back at force headquarters! Nothing more was heard.

The late autumn in 1989 brought significant flooding risk to a large area of my sub division. Severn beach and Aust were threatened by a combination of high tides and adverse winds, threatening overtopping of the sea defences in the area. We were particularly concerned regarding the Severn Rail Tunnel access point. I set to rewriting our operational plan in respect of flooding in the area. Luckily the plans had been drawn up by predecessors using much bitter experience and so for the most part my task was to check and update important contact details.

I was just starting to feel at home at Filton and enjoying the responsibility of my own command, when once again my career took another unexpected turn. In late November 1989, I received an instruction to report to the chief constable's office in Old Bridewell in central Bristol. I could not think what this was for, but was aware that the chief had been taking an interest in our emergency planning and so assumed that it was probably to discuss that aspect of my duty.

So it came as quite a shock when he congratulated me on my performance as sub-divisional commander at Filton, and then said that he was promoting me to the rank of superintendent at force headquarters. He went on to say that the Home Office had instructed all forces to take a heightened interest in staff development and appoint an officer at superintendent rank to head up a new 'Career Development' department that would administer an evidence-based annual report system for all staff.

It was planned that I would establish the new department with just myself and Mrs Janet Vardy, a senior administrator, but that I would eventually be joined by a chief inspector, an inspector and two additional civilian staff to assist me. The Career Development department would initially be located at Old Bridewell, but would soon move to the new force headquarters at Portishead, just outside Bristol. In addition to maintaining annual reports on all staff, I would also be required to examine reports on staff recommended for promotion, and prepare short lists for the chief constable's final selection.

At the conclusion of my interview with him, the chief grinned and said, "Now perhaps you will stop bothering me about a helicopter!" Little did he know!

15

Super-
intendent.

Force HQ

Upon taking up my new posting at headquarters, my first task was to set up this brand new department. This was going to be a totally new thing for me, it was personnel-related and not something that I had ever specialised in before, yet I was going to be the senior career advisor to all force employees, both service and civilian. The rules as published in a Home Office circular stated that I should provide a totally confidential advice service to all members of staff and administer and maintain all annual appraisals on all staff up to a very senior level.

The force's annual staff appraisal scheme had to be completely revised as soon as practicable and would now become an evidence-based system, reporting solely on the key skills and experience required to fulfil the post occupied by the person under review. And for the first time, the subject of the report would be able to see what had been said about their performance and given the opportunity to reply.

We realised very quickly that in order to comply with the Home Office circular we would have to redesign the way that the force establishment was distributed. Every division and department would have to be allocated post numbers for everyone allocated to them. Each member of staff would then appear on our computer as occupying a clearly identified post and, when moved from one post to another, it could only be done if the post they were moving to was vacant.

The real difficulty was that in order to properly and accurately report on an individual's performance in their role, there had to be an agreed assessment of the skills and abilities required to fill the post. Obviously, many posts would require the same skills and abilities for a number of its posts, but these would all have to be assessed and agreed not only by the senior members of the division, but also by the staff associations and, in the case of civilians, the unions too. This preparatory work would become highly specialised and I now realised why I had been allocated several additional members of staff to bring the new system into effect. Chief Inspector Bev Hope Bell and Inspector Graham Tonkinson soon joined me, plus two sergeants.

We desperately needed to locate an evidence-based career development computer programme and after much research Janet Vardy and myself travelled to Kent Constabulary who were perfecting a programme which matched our requirements exactly. The system was expensive to purchase but the force was in no position to argue and quickly agreed to its purchase.

The system proved to be robust and exactly matched our requirements. The designer had spent a great deal of time ensuring that Janet, who would administer the system, was properly up to speed with it, and we were soon ready to start loading up all the posts and post holders in the force. The system had to be loaded very carefully and that alone would take many weeks to accomplish, but eventually we not only had a system that identified every post in the force but also accounted for everyone the force employed. The system and numbers balanced!

The next phase was to train all supervisors in what was meant by evidence-based annual reporting. That was where all of the carefully assessed skills and abilities required for each post came in. We managed it and I am proud to say that due to my dedicated staff, the force was able to make use of a first-class annual appraisal scheme.

At the same time, I was re-organising our promotion board system, which featured interviews intended to examine performance of individuals whilst performing temporary duty in a higher rank. Each interview board then produced a list of successful candidates who were deemed suitable for future promotion.

With this new responsibility and a whole new department to establish, the air support project had to take a back seat for a while. However, I had remained in close contact with air support matters through the various regional and national air support committees that I had been appointed to. I was painfully aware that, apart from myself and the small band of air observers that I had established, no other senior officer within the force had picked up the torch and as a result air support was no longer being researched.

Yet, like every other force in the UK, we were suffering far greater instances of vehicle-related crime than had previously been the case. High-powered vehicles were being stolen almost every day and used either for dangerous joy riding or, even more seriously, as getaway cars in the commission of high-value crime.

In 1991, however, things took a dramatic turn for the better. The Home Office recognised that the small number of forces that had adopted air support in their fight against crime were showing a significant improvement in their prevention and detection of vehicle-related crime. As a result, it was announced that the government had set aside several million pounds sterling each year to encourage the establishment of full air support cover to police forces across England and Wales. Forces were told that provided they adhered to certain guidelines they could apply for grants of 51% of the cost of the purchase of a helicopter and other vital equipment. Plus agreed preferential loan rates for the remaining 49%.

The guidelines adhering to the new initiative were calculated to rapidly increase coverage and safety. In the first instance, preference would be given to applications submitted by two or more joint forces intending to operate together over a larger area. In recognition of the need for greater public and crew safety, all aircraft in police service, especially helicopters, would now be required to be multi-engined. A new Police Air Operators Certificate was established, providing very strict guidelines under which all police air operations must in future be conducted. These were the conditions that myself and others had been pushing for, for a long time!

In June 1991 we had again hired in a helicopter to support our policing of Pilton (Glastonbury) pop festival. I had managed to secure a further increase in the force air support budget which was now approaching an annual figure of £200,000. David Shattock, the chief constable, had requested an overview of the site to increase his appreciation of the situation.

I had long operated a policy of refusing jolly flights for senior officers, but on this occasion there was a clear opportunity to increase the chief's understanding of what air support could offer, and so immediately agreed, writing myself into the operational crew for the flight. In the event, the flight was very successful and during our time over the festival site we were able to assist one of our task force units that was having problems with making an arrest.

When we landed back at our base at Filton airfield, the chief thanked me for arranging his overview flight and then remarked, "I told you to stop all this in 1987, didn't I?" "Yes sir," I replied. "And I told you again in 1989!" "Yes sir!" "And I gave you a written instruction to stop in 1990." "Yes sir!" "And I suppose that if I told you again today, you wouldn't listen?" "No sir!" "Well done," he said and jumped in his car and drove off.

Later that year, my air support budget was again increased. However, the situation in respect of vehicle-related crime was continuing to cause much alarm. So much so that Assistant Chief Constable (Crime) Mike Hedges, called a conference of all senior officers at Kings Weston House (our local training school) to discuss the situation. Somewhat embarrassingly, just as the conference was ending it was discovered that the ACC's powerful Ford Escort Cosworth car had been stolen from the school's car park! His uniform was on the back seat. The car was later recovered from a field, minus its wheels and seats, his uniform was recovered nearby.

I had been in discussions with a contact in Gloucester Constabulary operations department for some time regarding the possibility of them joining with us in future air operations. I was very much aware that they too wanted air cover, but could not afford it. With their agreement, I submitted yet another report to Chief Constable David Shattock, requesting permission to submit a formal application to the Home Office for the necessary funding to buy and operate a helicopter jointly with Gloucester Constabulary, and to operate from Filton Airfield in support of policing in both constabulary areas.

This time attitudes had changed, crime was soaring and we had lost the initiative. Now at last air support was seen as a way of getting that initiative back where it should be – with us!

The chief, after consultation with the Police Authority, then instructed me to prepare the necessary documentation for his signature, in order to apply for Home Office funding for the project.

Two months later we received confirmation that our application had been successful and that we could start the process of finding a suitable pre-owned helicopter. Gloucester recognised Avon and Somerset had set the running, and possessed a great deal of the required ancillary equipment, and so agreed that we should take the lead in setting up the new unit. The split in financial input and in manpower would be on a two-thirds and one-third basis, which roughly matched our expected usage of the hours to be flown over each force area. The framework for the new unit was coming together!

I immediately commenced the search for a suitable used Twin Squirrel helicopter and our agent quickly discovered one in the south of France. The aircraft was an F2 version of the Aerospatial Twin Squirrel. It had been manufactured in 1991 and sold to an alpine tour company which within six months of taking delivery had gone bankrupt. As a result, the helicopter had spent the next 18 months sitting in a bank's compound, waiting for a decision to sell it. It had only flown for a total of 253 hours from new. It was like finding a used car for sale that had not even had its first service.

I quickly arranged for a full survey to be carried out and, following a very favourable report, requested both chief constables and their police authorities to agree to its purchase. The necessary permissions were soon in place and I was able to instruct our agent, Police Aviation Services (PAS) of Staverton Airport Gloucester, to purchase the helicopter on our behalf.

A few weeks later I had the pleasure one Friday evening to be at Staverton in time to see our very own aircraft landing for the first time in England. She was metallic bronze in colour and was bearing French registration letters F-GJAJ. However, she was now the property of the joint Air Support Consortium of Avon and Somerset and the Gloucestershire Forces.

The flight to England was just the first step of a very long and complicated process to convert the aircraft from a machine intended to take skiers and sightseers around the Alps into a well-equipped police aircraft. This was not just going to be a quick paint job!

The aircraft had to be totally converted to the police role. Sliding doors on both sides for quick exit from the rear seats, thermal image and long-range high definition TV cameras, full satellite navigation systems and high skids to enable landings in most terrains. Most essentially, she was to be fitted with the latest UHF and VHF police communications systems. Her French registration had been cancelled, and she now carried the British registration G-OASP. Finally, she underwent a total re-painting in our chosen red, white and blue paint scheme.

Sadly, despite this being the culmination of many years of intensive planning, I realised that as I was now a superintendent, I could never take command of the new unit that I was commissioning. Time had passed me by and the rank of the unit commander of police air support units had been set as that of inspector. Despite all my efforts, I was now too senior to be able to command such a unit!

Luckily, over the past few years while I had been building up the air support budget, I had gathered around me a small team of dedicated air support enthusiasts. Inspector Chris Ware, Sergeant Pete Sweet and constables Phil Scott and Peter Hickenbotham, had been key members of my team. All of them were true enthusiasts, and each one was especially skilled in the different aspects of what we were about.

Each one of the team concentrated on their particular specialisation whilst we developed our small part-time unit into one ready for full-time police air operations.

To assist with the task, we were now also joined by a sergeant and three constables from our partners the Gloucester force in order to increase our establishment.

Inspector Chris Ware became the unit executive officer, or UEO, the recognised name for UK Police Air Unit Commanders. The deputy UEO was the responsibility of the Gloucestershire force and their sergeant was therefore to assume that position. PC2982 Phil Scott was quite simply outstanding at all things electrical and complicated, and he concentrated on learning all of our new radio and satellite navigation systems together with the day and night surveillance equipment that the aircraft carried. Once he understood the new equipment, he took on the task of teaching everyone else. Peter Hickenbotham was the strong and steady influence that quietly assisted Chris in keeping everyone on task.

My role was now one of ensuring that anything that was needed from a managerial support position was always there. Following some discussion with both sets of chief officers, it was agreed that the name of our new unit would be the Western Counties Air Operations Unit, or WCAOU. We also commissioned a new unit badge which depicted the hat badge emblems of both forces, and appeared on both sides of the aircraft.

There remained, however, one final hurdle that we had to overcome before we could become a police air operations unit in our own right. That was the acquisition of a 'Police Air Operators Certificate' (PAOC) issued by the Civil Aviation Authority. Without that certificate, we would have to pay a specialist aviation company to operate the aircraft for us, and in so doing lose many of the advantages that ownership of our own aircraft provided.

However, before the CAA would issue with us with a PAOC they needed to be confident that we possessed properly trained and experienced pilots and observers, and had a proper maintenance contract in place to ensure the full and safe operation of the aircraft.

In simple terms, we had to show that we would be able to operate our aircraft to the same standards as that required of a small airline. Clearly we did not have that expertise within our consortium and so needed the assistance of an experienced chief pilot to guide us through that stage of our evolution.

Captain Ian (Pinger) Payne was appointed as our unit chief pilot. 'Pinger' had been a Lieutenant Commander in the Royal Navy, flying Sea

King anti-submarine helicopters. On leaving the navy, he had joined our existing specialist contractor, PAS, and since had flown with us on several occasions when we hired helicopters from them. He had quickly responded to our advert for a chief pilot and was able to join us almost immediately.

Ian's knowledge and experience became instrumental in bringing the new unit rapidly up to the very high standard of safety and efficiency required by the Civil Aviation Authority. The grant of our PAOC followed many months of hard work, much of it overseen by not only Pinger but by the other pilots that PAS had supplied to us on a contractual basis. It is true to say that the whole team at Western Counties worked tirelessly to achieve success.

By May 1995, we were clearly ready to commence full-time air operations. We had selected and trained a sufficient number of air observers to cover two shifts per day, seven days a week. Sufficient pilots had been engaged on contract from PAS to ensure that the unit would be operational from 8 am to 3.30 am in each 24-hour period. To have covered the full 24-hour period would have required far greater expenditure at a time when our budget was already fully extended.

But our aircraft was not ready! The vital TV and thermal imaging pod had been delivered late by the manufacturer, and as a result our contractor PAS had been unable to complete the complicated process of fitting and testing in time for our scheduled commencement date of the first of June. To make matters worse, Pilton pop festival was almost on us again.

Luckily PAS had a spare helicopter available, a Twin Squirrel G-PASE. She was similar to our own aircraft, but was an earlier F1 version with slightly less endurance and power.

The formal launch day arrived and was attended by chief officers and members of police authorities of both forces. Photographs were taken, short speeches were made and that was it, the Western Counties Air Operations Unit was up and running!

For me, it brought a very strange mixture of emotions. I had achieved the target that I had worked so hard for over ten years to create, yet at the very moment of it becoming a reality my involvement was at an end.

The unit quite rightly had its own commander, UEO Inspector Chris Ware. As the UEO, Chris was now in full charge and together with the chief constables of the two forces, was legally responsible for the conduct of the unit.

With no ongoing or line responsibility for the unit, I returned to my primary role of being the superintendent in charge of the force career development department. Obviously I called in quite frequently to see the guys on the air unit, and enjoyed their company on several social occasions, but that was the limit of my involvement.

Shortly after the launch of the unit, the chief constable offered me command of the Staplehill Division, but by then I had been away from operational matters for many years and as I was less than three years from retirement, I declined.

My final years in the service were spent visiting other forces, assisting with promotion boards and developing evidence-based annual reports.

By October 1998, it was time for me to retire and I gave notice of that fact to the new chief constable, Steve Pilkington.

It was a very strange feeling on my final day to hand over the warrant card that I had carried at all times for the past 30 years.

I was given a number of presents at my retirement party, including an impressive wooden base onto which were glued my truncheon, a pair of handcuffs and hat badges from my original Somerset and Bath Force and also one from the Avon and Somerset Force.

The Air Support Unit gave me a plaque onto which had been secured the collective control stick from a Bolkow BO105 helicopter.

That concluded my career as a police officer and, as I thought then, my involvement with the police service. But I was still only 53 years of age and was not ready to stand still for very long.

16

A Second Career

The first few weeks after my retirement from the police were a kaleidoscope of mixed emotions. There was a certain amount of relief about no longer having the responsibility of command in difficult firearms situations. But at the same time came the dawning realisation that I was now completely outside of the service that had governed and directed me for the past 30 years. I recalled hearing an old colleague telling me one day that, "There is nothing more ex than being an ex senior police officer!" And I realised just how true that was. Serving officers who I knew well, and who a few short weeks ago would have discussed all manner of things with me, suddenly became much more reticent. I was no longer a member of the family; it almost seemed that overnight I had become untrustworthy! I soon got used to it but it did hurt for a while.

There was also the problem of my own immediate future. Police officers were normally expected to retire on completing 30 years service. It was at that point that their maximum pension was achieved. To remain in service after that point would mean that significant pension contributions would still be deducted from salary, but the pension itself would no longer increase. My 30 year anniversary was the 18th October 1998.

With that factor in mind, I had been talking to the managing director of Police Aviation Services, Mark Trumble, who I knew well from working with him over the past few years. He had indicated to me that there would be a job for me at PAS after I retired, lecturing in their observer training school. This was a very attractive proposition for me and had encouraged me to give three months' notice of my intention to retire at the end of October 1998. However, two months after submitting that notice I had received an apologetic phone call from Mark, informing me that he had just sold the company to Bombardier Aviation from Belfast, and they did not intend to continue with the training school. The job was therefore no longer open to me. I was devastated, but could not at that point withdraw my resignation.

Because I had been expecting to start with PAS I had not explored any other options in respect of future employment, so for a while I busied myself with re-decorating the house and other previously neglected DIY tasks in the garden. But I was becoming increasingly frustrated at having no real purpose in life. I had to do something, but what?

Then suddenly, out of the blue, I received a phone call from David Lewis at McAlpine Helicopters in Kidlington, Oxfordshire. He invited me to come up to see himself and Dick Richardson, the general manager. He explained that they might have a job for me that would last for about six months. It sounded interesting and I immediately agreed to go up and see them.

I had known McAlpine Helicopters for almost as long as I had known PAS because during my research into the concept of police aviation, both companies had assisted me greatly. PAS had favoured the German Bolkow helicopters and were now the UK agent for the new MD 900 helicopter built by the American McDonnell company. McAlpine Helicopters, part of the McAlpine Construction corporation, had always specialised in the French Aerospatiale helicopter machines such as the Squirrel, but were now the main agent for the combined French and German Eurocopter EC135 helicopter.

I drove up to McAlpines just a few days later and saw Dick Richardson and David Lewis. I knew David very well and had previously met Dick during my many previous visits to the company.

They explained that they intended to promote the new EC135 to the police service as the most efficient and reliable police helicopter available anywhere in the world. At the same time, they recognised that they were in direct competition with PAS who were promoting the MD900 helicopter.

They were looking for someone who would be prepared to travel to police forces all over the country, concentrating initially on those who had air support units, to establish a good rapport with the units and to discuss with them their current and future requirements in respect of aircraft and also role equipment. They believed that I was the person that could best fulfil that role and they offered me an initial contract for six months. I would be expected to work a minimum of five days per month at a very favourable daily rate. The minimum of five days per month could be extended on occasions for a special task and I would also be expected to represent them during conferences and exhibitions at the same rate. It was a dream opportunity for me and I readily accepted their offer. It was agreed that I would commence my work for them in January 1999.

It became evident that it was to be left to my own discretion which police forces I would visit on the five days that I was expected to work for McAlpines, so I started ringing around the units, booking in visits on days that suited them. Generally speaking, they were quite happy to see me and very happy that McAlpines had employed a retired air support-minded person to act as their liaison person. The only unit that was unwilling to receive me was the Manchester Air Operations unit, who being a PAS/MD 900 operator were clearly suspicious of our motive.

That first month, in January 1999, I visited North Wales, North Midlands, Dyfed Powys, West Midlands and Suffolk ASUs. They were all very open with me and happy to discuss the full range of issues ranging from problems with McAlpines' maintenance, their aircraft or very often improvements required in the role equipment fitted to their particular machine. At the end of the month, I submitted a six-page report to McAlpines summarising what I had learned, and making suggestions regarding what actions we should take.

The next month visits were made to Devon and Cornwall, Wiltshire, Surrey, the Metropolitan Police at their Lippets Hill base and finally South Wales Police ASU at Cardiff. Once again, a full report was submitted at the end of the month.

My activities continued each month and gradually I ranged further afield, visiting units in Belfast, Northern Ireland, the Strathclyde unit in Glasgow, the Humberside unit at RAF Leconfield, the West Yorkshire unit at Cartgate on the M1, the Sheffield unit based at Sheffield Police traffic HQ, the Central Counties unit at Halfpenny Green Airfield at Bobbington South Staffordshire, the East Midlands unit based at Sulby near Welford Northamptonshire, the Essex Police Unit at Borham, and finally the Dorset Police unit based near the Winfrith nuclear power station in Dorset. A great deal of intelligence was gained for McAlpines but at the same time adding considerably to my own knowledge of a policing method that was rapidly gaining in importance.

When I first started as McAlpines police liaison consultant, there were three main aircraft in service with UK police forces. The old BO105 Bolkow had been all but phased out of service, and was now only used as a spare by PAS. The most common aircraft was still the Aerospatiale AS 355 Twin Squirrel helicopter either in F2 or the more powerful N variant. However, the Squirrel itself was gradually being replaced by the much more advanced EC135 helicopter which was the product of the new Eurocopter company based at Donauworth in Germany.

Eurocopter had been created by the amalgamation of Germany's Messerschmitt Bolkow Blohm Company with the French Aerospatiale Company. Ultimately it was part of Airbus Industries and was the largest helicopter manufacturing company in the world.

Both manufacturing bases had been retained by Eurocopter as they tended to specialise in different types of machine.

The Aerospatiale company at their base in Marignane in the south of France had specialised in small corporate helicopters like the Squirrel which they produced in both single- and twin-engined versions. In addition, they also produced the larger Dauphine machine, which was developing a great reputation with both corporate and military customers, and had proved to be an efficient and rapid search and rescue helicopter. Finally, they also produced the large Puma military transport helicopter in use by the RAF and other European armed services.

Messerschmitt Bolkow Blohm specialised in smaller twin-engined battlefield and scout-type helicopters which had proved to be highly successful in tough operating conditions. They had been adopted by UK police forces operating outside of the Metropolitan Police area, and in the early days of UK police air operations had built up a strong reputation for reliability and durability. The BO105 design was, by the late 1990s, showing its age and as a result MBB had introduced their advanced new twin-engined helicopter the EC135, designed specifically for the emergency services. The new machine featured a shrouded 'Fenestron'-type tail rotor which was an advanced safety feature for a machine which might be required to land in rough terrain.

The EC135 was the machine that Eurocopter, through their agent McAlpines, was promoting as the ideal helicopter for UK police forces to standardise on. It was clear that they saw my appointment as an ideal opportunity to focus attention on the new machine. It was especially important because the introduction of the EC135 had coincided with another new machine, the McDonnell Douglas MD900 Explorer.

The new MD Explorer was a twin-engined machine with good performance. It too had been designed specifically for military and emergency services use like the EC135. Uniquely, it featured a totally new type of directional control system called the NOTAR (No Tail Rotor).

The NOTAR system replaced the conventional helicopter tail rotor with a powerful jet of air produced by an integral fan adjacent to the engines. This powerful fan directed high pressure air through the hollow tail boom to a moveable directional nozzle at the end of the tail. The pilot could alter the thrust direction of the nozzle and as a result could control the attitude and direction of the aircraft.

Helicopters are not normally the quietest form of transport, but many people do not understand that a very high proportion of the noise of a helicopter is created not by the engine, but by the tail rotor. The small blades on a conventional helicopters tail rotor have to rotate at very high speed to provide the necessary thrust in order to control its direction. The small size of the blades mean that the tips of the blades are moving at or near the speed of sound, hence the noise!

The designers of both the EC135 and the McDonnell Explorer had sought to eliminate the root cause of the noise in different ways. Eurocopter, by redesigning the tail rotor to become multi bladed and enclosed in a Fenestron shroud. In contrast, the McDonnell company had opted to eliminate the tail rotor altogether, by creating their NOTAR system. Both systems were similarly effective in reducing the noise of the aircraft.

It became immediately clear that both aircraft engendered a strong feeling of protective loyalty amongst the units that operated them. This was especially true amongst those units that used pilots supplied under contract from either McAlpines or PAS. This was a quite understandable situation and only to be expected. Nevertheless, despite obviously coming from McAlpines, the vast majority of the PAS Explorer operators were happy to receive visits from me on a regular basis, and to openly discuss operational and equipment challenges that we all faced. The only unit that remained closed to me for many years was Manchester, although even they too eventually accepted my visits.

As time went on and my knowledge of police aviation in general greatly increased, I was often asked to attend conferences in Britain and Europe to give presentations on the UK system, I was naturally a strong advocate of our approved air support unit infrastructure and national policies. One such lecture was delivered at the 2004 Paris Air Show.

In 2005, McAlpine helicopters, previously part-owned by Eurocopter, became wholly owned by Eurocopter. The McAlpine name disappeared and the company became Eurocopter UK. I was at first concerned as to how that might affect me, but it merely widened my scope of influence and I found myself visiting air support units in France, Germany and Holland as well as the UK units. By now I was also making regular visits to the Police Service of Northern Ireland's air unit base at Aldergrove.

PSNI had been operating a Britten-Norman Islander twin turbine fixed-wing aircraft for many years, and their UEO Roger McConnell and his deputy Brian Cairns had attended an air support conference in the UK.

We had been talking in the bar one evening and it became obvious that one of the main reasons that they were at the conference was that they were looking at the possibility of extending PSNI's air operations to include use of a helicopter. Obviously I was very keen to promote that development and arranged to visit them at Aldergrove. That first visit was the start of a close relationship that was to develop over many years.

But I am perhaps moving on too quickly. Paula and I had started our married life back in 1969 with almost no financial security. Both of our fathers had died some years before and our mothers were managing but were certainly not well off. My take home pay as a young police officer were less than £65 per month, and Paula, although working hard, was not well paid either. So as a result our marriage had been a small affair and our honeymoon very short. It is true to say that it was Paula's savings that created our home and what we put in it. She was the true star of our family's well-being.

However, despite the fact that my career had been quite successful, and I had received regular promotions, we had never been in a position to enjoy expensive holidays, preferring instead to provide a happy and stable family life for our three children, Julie, Jeremy and Esme. But now, having retired from the service at the end of 1998 and having started a new career as a consultant to McAlpines, I planned that Paula and I would embark on a once in a lifetime round the world flying vacation. By the time I retired, the children were older and able to look after themselves, so with the assistance of a travel agent friend I planned a two-month holiday, flying westbound around the world. The cost of the trip, using either British Airways or Quantas and their allied airlines, actually worked out surprisingly inexpensive.

Koala | © Kangaroo Island Seasons

17

Around the World in 80 days

My travel agent friend, John Stevens of Compass Travel, had advised booking one night's accommodation on arrival in each country to be visited and thereafter booking further accommodation wherever we found ourselves. Car hire had been arranged in advance. I had made contact with police air units in several of the countries we were intending to visit and that ultimately proved to be very helpful.

And so it was that on the 14th January 2001 Paula and I boarded a jumbo jet at Heathrow and flew off on our big adventure. John Stevens had recommended a westbound route as that was less likely to result in any jet lag, and our subsequent experience proved his advice to be well founded. Our first stop was in Los Angeles where we had booked a hotel in the Marina Del Rey district close to Santa Monica Boulevard. Then we took a tourist bus around Hollywood and saw the spectacular homes of many film stars.

Finally, that first evening we walked along the Venice Beach walkway from Santa Monica Boulevard to our hotel, the Marina Del Rey. It was daylight when we started walking, but it was a long way and as the light started to fail I began to feel quite vulnerable. I was carrying a video camera and an expensive 35mm camera over my shoulder. I noticed several groups of threatening looking youngsters hanging about which heightened my concern. I was very relieved to get back to the hotel before it became completely dark. The staff were incredulous that we had taken such a risk, but we simply had not realised the danger when we set off. Apparently, no one should risk walking that route in the evening gloom! It was suggested that we only got away with it because we looked such an inviting target that we must have been part of a police trap. Lesson learned!

The following day we visited the Universal Film Studios and watched some spectacular staged demonstrations. Later in the afternoon we were passing through a part of the city where a road had been closed in order to facilitate a scene for a film being made. The street closure was being enforced by a police motorcyclist stationed at either end of the street. I noticed that both officers, although wearing full uniform including side arms, looked older than myself and somewhat intrigued I decided to speak to one of them.

I explained that I was a retired English police officer and asked what their retirement age was. He laughed and said, "Oh, I've been retired for several years now, but after we retire we keep our uniform and kit for many years, and when they have a job like this they ask us to do it and pay us. It gives us a supplementary income, and saves using serving officers on minor tasks." What a good idea!

On the morning of our last day in Los Angeles I had arranged to make a visit to the Los Angeles Police Department's air support base. Paula decided not to accompany me. I arrived at the downtown base at about 11 am and was immediately shown to their lecture theatre where I saw a film about the work of the unit. It was clear that they possessed quite a few aircraft, but I was less than impressed by the fact that they were clearly happy to patrol the city area at fairly low level using single-engined Bell 206 helicopters.

The role equipment carried by their aircraft, such as the dedicated police air-to-ground radio, the powerful searchlight and the public address speakers, did not appear as advanced as our own, and overall I was disappointed by what I saw. The pilots were recognised as serving police officers, but it was evident that most had joined as pilots from the armed services, and had never actually performed normal policing duty on the streets. In truth, they were specialist police aviators rather than being fully experienced police officers.

They were amazed when I explained to them that in the UK the CAA had ruled that police pilots had to be professional pilots with a minimum of 1,500 hours' experience. They were employed as civilians to fly police aircraft and were not police officers.

I further explained that the CAA had ruled that police officers were not allowed to fly police aircraft. They questioned why that should be, and I explained that in the UK the CAA believed that there was a dangerous clash of interests in allowing a police officer to fly the aircraft. It was feared that the police officer might become so engrossed in making an arrest, that he could ignore the primary task of flying safely. There was also the fact that all police aircraft in the UK were now highly complex twin-turbine helicopters, and very few serving officers in the UK were skilled enough to fly them.

I was quite disappointed by my visit to the LA Police Air Operations unit. I was expecting to find a much greater level of commitment to aviation safety than I discovered. They were clearly providing a good level of service to the officers on the ground, but somehow I just didn't feel the level of determination or professionalism that UK units possessed.

But now it was time to resume our adventure and later that evening we took a taxi to Los Angeles International Airport to fly on to Fiji. We boarded a fairly elderly Boeing 747-200 jumbo jet of Air Pacific Airways. To say that the cabin was crowded was an understatement, but the cabin crew were smart and dressed in Polynesian-style uniforms.

The aircraft taxied out to the runway and after a few moments started its take-off run. The acceleration was not that fast and the run seemed to go on for ages but finally just as I was getting quite worried it managed to climb into the air with quite a lot of vibration and noise. But at least we were up!

After about an hour I noticed that we were still only at about 28,000 feet which, although not worrying, was considerably lower than my previous experience of long-distance flights in the 747. Just then, the captain came on the intercom and his announcement was quite amusing, it went something like this.

"Good evening, ladies and gentlemen and welcome to this Air Pacific flight to Nandi airport on Fiji. This is a very long flight and is scheduled to take about 15 hours. What makes it a little different is that we will be crossing the international date line in the reverse direction and so that instead of landing tomorrow afternoon it will be the day after. You will lose a day of your life but I am afraid the company are not prepared to compensate you for that. Also, some of you will have noticed that I am still only flying at 28,000 feet, that is because we have a full passenger load tonight, and as it is such a long flight I am carrying the maximum amount of fuel that we can cram in. At the moment, I just cannot get any higher, but as soon as we burn off a little more fuel I will go up to about 39,000 feet." It was all very jovial and he was clearly revelling in being able to say it.

The aircraft was certainly not in its first flush of youth, but the crew were enthusiastic and helpful and overall it was a very pleasant but very long flight.

We landed at Nandi the following afternoon and made our way to the arrivals area. The airport itself was very small and the buildings quite basic, but the welcome was wonderful with beaming staff and much calling out of "Bula bula" (welcome). We were headed for the Royal Denaroo Resort Hotel, one of the finest on Fiji, but the bus we boarded was an old bone shaker with a badly cracked windscreen. The condition of the bus was quickly explained as soon as we got onto the main roads away from the airport.

The roads were full of large deep potholes and most of the other traffic was farm tractors pulling huge trailers filled with sweetcorn plants recently harvested. The journey was quite an experience!

After what seemed an age, but was probably only about 45 minutes, we arrived at the hotel itself which was quite stunning. Built in a very open-plan style from a dark wood, the reception area was opulent and staffed by huge Fijian porters who whisked our luggage away to our room whilst we booked in.

We had been allocated a wonderful cabin just off the beach in a coconut grove. The hut had what appeared to be a straw roof and had been designed to look like a native Fijian hut. It was beautifully furnished inside. We were very happy and soon experienced bathing in a sea which was much warmer than we had ever experienced before.

Fiji has a very strange population mix of local indigenous Fijians who comprise about 60% of the population, the remainder being of Pakistan extraction. The Fijians appear to be very happy and welcoming, but at the same time are very laid back with a sort of 'manyana' attitude to life. As a result, the much more business-oriented Pakistan community appear to be taking a very strong grip on commerce and there are some tensions between the two communities which occasionally surface. A second complicating factor is the rigid caste system present within the Pakistan community. At the lower caste level there is much poverty evident and many people live in very deprived circumstances.

It was that latter situation which had caused Paula and I to visit Fiji as part of our tour. Rotary International, through its Worldwide Foundation programme, had become very much aware of the terrible living conditions that some people were experiencing in some of the deprived areas in Fiji. The conditions were each year exacerbated during the hurricane season when many of the poor conditioned living huts were blown down or simply blown away. As a result, Rotary International had developed steel-framed alloy homes known as Rotorhomes. These sturdy homes were designed to be hurricane-proof and their frames were driven into the ground to such an extent that they were capable of resisting the most extreme weather. Rotary clubs all around the world had been encouraged to donate the cost of building Rotorhomes and my club had enthusiastically responded.

Within a relatively short time, the club was advised that the Bristol East Avon Rotorhome had been built and was already occupied. During our planning for our round the world trip, Paula and I had decided to visit Fiji quite independently. However, as soon as the club realised that we were going to be close to their donated home they immediately asked if we could try to locate the community where the home had been established, and to visit it and report back. We happily agreed.

The Rotary Charity on Fiji was organised by an incredible man, Peter Drysdale, who had taken over the local administration of the Rotorhomes project. He also organised the efficient distribution of clothing and foodstuffs donated by Rotarians, mainly from New Zealand and Australia. Rotary International had put me in contact with him prior to our arrival in Fiji, and within a couple of days he visited us at our hotel and invited us to accompany him on one of his regular distribution runs. We both climbed into his large but very battered Toyota pick-up truck and drove off into the hills above Nandi, the main town near the hotel. The back of the truck was loaded with donated clothing.

It was already the rainy season and the dirt tracks were very muddy but Peter obviously knew the area very well and it was clear that we were in safe hands. About every mile or so we would come up upon small settlements, usually of very dilapidated wooden huts, but also occasionally, a few metal-skinned Rotorhomes that were obviously much newer. As soon as we arrived in a community, people would cluster around and Peter would be handing out supplies of clothing and food. What did amaze Paula and I was the sheer quality of some of the clothing that was being distributed, so much so that I commented to Peter about it. He grinned and explained that Rotary in New Zealand and Australia was still a little more select than it had become in some other parts of the world. He said that as a result, Rotarians and their wives in New Zealand and Australia might well purchase the latest designer wear, but only wear it a couple of times before handing it in to the charity collection. That same designer wear then ended up in the back of his truck being handed out to very poor people in Fijian villages. I think that Paula was quite envious of some of the clothing now being worn in very muddy conditions!

At about lunchtime, we arrived at a small cluster of huts quite high up in the hills. Most of the huts were very battered indeed but one was a newly built Rotorhome. It bore a metal plate describing it as a Rotorhome donated by Bristol East Avon Rotary Club. My club! We met the occupants who were fairly elderly, but were accompanied by a large family all living in the same hut. At least eight people living in quite a small area. Peter introduced us and the family were obviously very happy to see us. They insisted on us taking tea with them and, not wishing to offend, I accepted their offer. Then I was horrified to see the tea being prepared. There was an open log fire outside the hut and on top of the fire there was a blackened saucepan of what appeared to be boiling milk. Someone grabbed a handful of tea leaves and threw it in the pot, stirred it vigorously and poured the liquid into some tin mugs. I am not a tea drinker anyway, but the thought of drinking that made my stomach turn over, but they were all looking at me. I learned then that you can manage to drink it if you disengage brain before opening your mouth. It was awful but I managed to smile and thank them. I was very grateful when Peter said it was time to go!

Our stay on Fiji was quite short and within four days we were boarding a Quantas 767 and flying out to Auckland, New Zealand.

Once again I had planned ahead and made contact with the Auckland Police Air Support unit based at Mechanics Bay air base just outside Auckland itself.

Our flight from Fiji arrived at Auckland Airport in the middle of the afternoon, and as we made our way out of the arrivals concourse I was amazed to see a tall and smartly dressed NZ police officer standing there holding a large notice with the title 'Mr and Mrs Allinson' written on it. He introduced himself as Garry Lansing, a senior constable with the Auckland Police Air Unit. He explained that, as I had requested, they had booked me into the Roselawn Quality Hotel for two nights, and that the hotel was situated near the air unit at Mechanics Bay. They had realised that our flight was arriving during the afternoon rush hour and that we might have some difficulty in finding our way through the unfamiliar traffic. With that in mind, two of them had come out to the airport to meet us. Garry explained that he intended to drive us in our hired car to the hotel where he would be collected by his colleague, leaving us to settle in. Before leaving, he said that they would be expecting us at the air unit at 10 am the following morning and that they had planned an interesting day for us.

Their plan worked perfectly and Paula and I settled into a beautiful room with a wonderful view of the Auckland Tower through the window. As the evening grew dark, the tower was spectacularly lit up. It was one of those evenings that we would never forget.

The following morning, after a great breakfast in the hotel, we drove down to Mechanics Bay and found the police air unit next door to a quite large airborne emergency search and rescue unit, run jointly by the NZ ambulance service and Westpac, a big financial banking corporation.

The search and rescue unit was equipped with two fairly large BK 117 helicopters. There was a great deal of additional equipment in the compound, and it was evident that the search and rescue unit was very well supported.

The police Twin Squirrel helicopter was parked alongside the two larger helicopters but was also very clean and carried much the same equipment as similar units in the UK.

We were given a very interesting tour of the combined base and then the unit commander commenced giving us a safety briefing. It quickly became obvious to my surprise and pleasure that they intended to take us both up on a flight. This was indeed the case and we departed in what turned out to be a very spectacular flight over the city of Auckland and then out over the wooded territory to the southwest of the city. The coastline there was spectacularly and beautifully rugged.

The flight lasted about one hour and when we landed back at Mechanics Bay they suggested that we might like to take a light lunch at a nearby cafe and then come back to the unit at 2 pm because they had another surprise for us. I was intrigued but had no idea what was to follow.

The afternoon proved to be even more exciting than the morning! I had realised that Auckland was soon to host the Admirals Cup Yacht races, due the following weekend. But what I had not realised was just what a huge event the Admirals Cup was. The whole of the Auckland Bay marinas, docks and waterfront areas were full of yachts of all shapes and sizes, some of them clearly competitors and others more like floating palaces. The combined value must have run into billions of dollars. Auckland police carried the responsibility for crime reduction and for maintaining security over the entire event. To assist in waterborne security, the NZ national bank had provided them with a fleet of about 12 very high speed RIBs. These very powerful launches carried a normal crew of about six officers. There was a cabin on the main deck and a raised 'flying bridge' where the captain could steer from. Behind his position on the raised section, were three curved backrests allowing crew members to stand upright whilst being strapped securely in position by safety belts. The launch was powered by two very large and clearly very powerful outboard motors. We were going out on patrol in one of these high-speed launches!

Paula was shown to the enclosed cabin and I was allocated one of the standing positions on the top deck. I ensured that the strap around my waist was very tight. We left the quiet waters surrounding the air unit and quickly built up to an impressive speed. The g-force experienced as the captain gave a demonstration of its high-speed manoeuvrability was quite something.

I have never ever suffered from motion sickness but I could easily imagine that to be on board for a long time at such speeds would be very testing. We were there to patrol the lines of high-value yachts, and as soon as we arrived at the marina area we slowed down to a more respectable pace. Some of the locations around the coastal area of Auckland were really impressive and once again Paula and I had reason to be most grateful to Auckland police for the incredible welcome they gave us, and the wonderful way in which we were received. Sadly I don't think that any UK police force would have been able to go to such an effort as they did.

After offering our grateful thanks to Garry and the officers at Mechanics Bay, we left and enjoyed a second night in the Roselawn Hotel. There I secured a small book listing other quality hotels throughout New Zealand. This book was to become very important to us during the next two weeks as we toured both the North and South Islands of New Zealand. It became our practice at about 3 pm each day to work out where we would be at the end of the day's drive, and to look up the nearest quality hotel to that location, and then use my mobile phone to book a room and an evening meal. It never failed!

On leaving Auckland, we headed northwest towards the Bay of Islands and Whangarei. This area, known as the Cradle of a Nation, has many important historical sites and is held by the indigenous Maori people as being of significant importance. The Treaty of Waitangi was signed there in 1840.

The Treaty of Waitangi is the document that founded and created New Zealand as a sovereign nation. The treaty was signed by 45 Maori chiefs and by the representative of the British government, Lt Governor William Hobson, who thereafter became the first governor of New Zealand. The treaty, however, has remained controversial ever since then, and it is fair to say that the two parties to the treaty had differing expectations of what it provided.

For Paula and I, however, the area was quite magical in its beauty, and we were sad to leave the area in order to continue our brief exploration of New Zealand. We routed back down through Auckland to Hamilton and across to Rotorua where we visited the hot sulphur springs and geysers. Unlike the beautiful countryside that we had passed through before, neither of us were impressed by Rotorua. The sulphur smell was very strong and the impressive hot springs were almost impossible to view because of the sheer numbers of Japanese tourists all pushing to the front and taking pictures of each other – it was bedlam and we didn't stay very long.

In contrast, our next stop was at Lake Taupo on the Central Plateau. The drive there had been beautiful and the roads very quiet. The lake itself was so blue and was fed by many quite fast-flowing rivers. Once again, quite beautiful! It seemed that almost everywhere we went in rural New Zealand the surroundings were quite breathtaking. We lost count of the number of times that we said, "It can't get any more beautiful than this!" and then we would round a bend and it did. Whanganui National Park was stupendous and I would have wanted to spend more time there, but I was rapidly coming to the conclusion that I had miscalculated the amount of time that we had allocated to New Zealand, just two weeks. I don't think two months would have been too much.

Our next planned area to visit was Hawkes Bay and again NZ did not fail us. We had arranged to stay with the parents of one of the Rotary students at Bristol University that I acted as councillor to, Judith Watson. Her parents, Joy and Kevin, lived just outside Napier in a lovely house set in stunning gardens. They took great delight in showing us around the area and again we would have loved to have explored further, but were due in Wellington the next day to stay with Judith herself. After her studies in Bristol, Judith had returned to New Zealand and was now a teacher at a primary school just outside Wellington. She had a flat overlooking Wellington Harbour and we were to stay with her for one night before catching the ferry to start our tour of the South Island. She showed us the impressive New Zealand government buildings and then took us to the hills above Wellington where we had fantastic views of the surrounding coastline.

The following day we drove our hire car to the ferry port and handed it in to the hire company office. Whatever car hire company you use in New Zealand they all maintain a similar system which retains their fleet in the island that it was hired in. We had booked a car in Auckland on the day of our arrival on the North Island. But now as we were leaving the North Island we had to leave that car in Wellington and collect a similar car on arriving at Picton on the South Island.

The crossing of the Cook Strait was very smooth, although it can be very testing in bad weather. However, the relatively short crossing is just a small part of the journey between the two islands. Picton, the port of arrival on South Island, is only reached after a very long passage down a spectacular fjord-like river. The passage down that fjord took at least twice as long as the actual crossing of the Cook Strait, and on each side of the fjord was some of the most beautiful countryside imaginable.

Our replacement hire car was waiting for us on the quay and we were quickly on our way for our first planned night stop on the South Island. It was to be in the Blenheim and Marlborough area, one of New Zealand's wine growing regions. It was the first day of February and my birthday so we enjoyed a lovely meal in the restaurant of our quality hotel in Blenheim.

Our next stop was Kaikoura, a small coastal town well known for offering spectacular whale watching boat trips. Our tight schedule didn't allow us enough time to do that, but we did enjoy clambering over the rocky foreshore and getting a very close look at a number of seals laying amongst the rocks.

From Kaikura and Canterbury we headed across country to pick up Arthur's Pass towards Greymouth on the northwest coastline. We had been told that the Arthur's Pass route was spectacular but I don't think that either of us realised just how wild and beautiful it was. New Zealand was doing it again! Just when we didn't believe it could get any more beautiful it just did. There were some stunning lakes and creeks, very little traffic on the roads, except at one point when we were climbing up into the central highlands we kept seeing vintage Bugatti sports cars coming the other way. It must have been some sort of owners' club rally.

Whilst the journey over Arthur's Pass and the transalpine route over the Southern Alps to Greymouth had been really memorable, Greymouth itself was a disappointment. It certainly lived up to its name. In its early days it had been a small port exporting products from various mining activities in the area. As a result of its industrial background, it was now looking a bit grey and tired. However, the quality inn we found there was cheerful and welcoming and again had a very good restaurant.

But now it was time to head off southwest down the coastal route through fjordland past the Franz Josef and Fox Glaciers and in the high ground was always Mount Cook, so wild and imposing, to Central Otago's Lake Wanaka.

We spent a fabulous afternoon and evening at Lake Wanaka and witnessed the long white cloud over the lake.

That vision sums up New Zealand, the land of the long white cloud.

The next day we arrived in the southern tourist magnet of Queenstown. This beautiful flower-bedecked town is now the main stopping-off centre for every imaginable adventure tourism experience possible. You can go bungee jumping from impossibly high bridges. Speed boat riding on the 'Shotover Jet' on Lake Wakatipu, mountain climbing or just hiking. There is so much to do. We could easily have spent several days there but I realised that if we were to reach Milford Sound, one of my main objectives, we had to press on.

Our next night stop was at Lake Te Anau on the route to Milford Sound. For both of us, Te Anau was another of the most memorable places we visited on our entire trip. The little town was both tranquil and beautiful and the lake the bluest we had ever seen. The town was the centre of small tourist floatplane fights and I loved watching them coming and going every hour or so.

Sadly, our visit to Milford Sound was a huge anti-climax and disappointment. We had driven for a couple of hours northeast from Te Anau in lovely bright weather towards Milford Sound and then entered the very long road tunnel which passed through the high Alps to emerge above Milford Sound itself. But to our dismay, on emerging from the tunnel we were enveloped in very damp thick mist. It was very hard to pick out the road ahead.

We made it to the main water from in the Sound but we could see almost nothing. To make matters even worse, the area was buzzing with thousands of midges that made it impossible to stay outside the car. We didn't stay long before heading back towards Te Anau.

Essentially, that was almost the end of our wonderful visit to New Zealand. Had I done my homework better and had realised just what a beautiful country it was, we would have wanted to stay there longer. As it was, we now had to get to Christchurch to catch our flight to Australia.

We spent two days in Christchurch riding the trams around the city centre and enjoying the lovely central park before returning our car to the airport centre and catching a Quantas 767 to Sydney.

Our arrival in Sydney was unforgettable but not in a pleasant way. It was a lovely day, not a cloud in the sky and light winds too, but something went badly wrong with our landing.

The aircraft hit the runway very hard indeed and for a short moment bounced back into the air again, before hitting the runway a second time. Suddenly all the emergency oxygen masks fell from their overhead stowage and all you could see was hundreds of these masks dangling throughout the cabin.

As we taxied to the terminal, the passenger in front of me stood up and tried to pack his oxygen mask back in its housing but a stewardess approached saying, "Don't bother with that sir, this is a dockyard job!"

Paula was quite shaken, but bravely asked, "Who was doing the landing, someone on work experience?"

For us on this occasion, Sydney was only an interim stop because we were taking an internal fight to Adelaide.

On arrival at Adelaide we collected our hire car and drove to the historic suburb of Glenelg where my old friends Rod and Patsy Ferrier lived. They had kindly arranged to put us up in their spacious seafront home for a few days, and went out of their way to show us around the historic city of Adelaide and the beautiful hills overlooking the city.

The suburb of Glenelg also has a very interesting history, and was the place where many original British immigrants to South Australia first set foot on Australian soil. There is a lovely vintage tram service providing a link to the centre of Adelaide.

We rested with Rod and Patsy for a couple of days and then set off on the next part of our adventure, driving around the Spencer Gulf coastal route to Port Lincoln. There we had arranged to stay with Bruce and Irene Bennett who had been my Port Lincoln hosts during the GSE visit eight years previously. The drive to Port Lincoln took three days, but it was quite an eye opener for Paula as it was her first experience of crossing through remote outback territory on the way to Port Lincoln.

We had a really wonderful time with Bruce and Irene who took us sailing in their big motor cruiser around the small islands surrounding the Port Lincoln coastal area. The seas were crystal clear and I enjoyed a lot of swimming in warm water there. One small problem occurred when I forgot that I had put the electronic key for the hire car in the pocket of my swimming trunks. It, of course, got totally waterlogged and never worked properly after that, and I had to open the car doors manually using the key.

All too soon it was time to drive back around the Spencer Gulf, through Whyalla, Port Augusta and Port Pirie, to Gawler, where we would spend a few days with Brian and Anne Burt who had led the Australian group study exchange team to England shortly before I took our team to South Australia.

Brian knew the Barossa wine growing region well, and so we had a great time with him visiting wineries and sampling one or two glasses of their finest!

It was soon time to move on again and the next stage of our plan had always been to drive to Melbourne via the Great Ocean Road. This route proved to be just as spectacular as we had expected. The views in many places were incredible and I often had to remind myself to concentrate on my driving rather than sight seeing. We saw the 'Twelve Apostles' coastal rock formations and stopped at Cape Otway, the southernmost point in Australia.

This region was quite heavily forested with large eucalyptus trees. The eucalyptus is, of course, the home to the koala, many of whom were to be seen sleeping in the trees or occasionally taking a snack.

After our beautiful drive around the great ocean road, Melbourne seemed chaotic and I was grateful to be able to park our hire car in the hotel car park and to make use of Melbourne's modern tram system to view the city. It was a very strange mix of modern and semi-Victorian styles. Our stay was short, because we were booked into a Sydney hotel for three days before flying up to Cairns for the final part of the Australian section of our trip.

The drive from Melbourne towards Sydney was fine but lacked the impressive views that had marked the Adelaide to Melbourne section. Except, however, the small town of Holbrook, New South Wales. What set Holbrook apart from other small townships was that right in the middle of the town, in a large well-tended grassy park, was a full-sized submarine! But Holbrook was nowhere near the sea! This was clearly worthy of investigation, so we stopped and went over to the submarine, which had a number of information boards displayed close by. What had appeared to be a complete submarine was actually only the part of the submarine's casing and conning tower that would have been seen when it was on the surface of the sea. Then I remembered that In Australia and New Zealand, war memorials were very often preserved tanks, guns, aircraft and occasionally ships like the Corvette Whyalla that we had previously seen preserved in Whyalla.

Holbrook had originally been called Germanton. However, at the end of the Great War there was a great deal of anti-German sentiment in Australia, and the town council took the decision to change the name of their town. They decided to honour the name of Lt Norman Douglas Holbrook RN, who had won the Victoria Cross in a submarine whilst assisting Australian troops at Gallipoli.

In 1995, the Royal Australian Navy heard that Holbrook was seeking to erect a suitable war memorial appropriate to the name Holbrook, and offered them the recently decommissioned Oberon class submarine, HMAS Otway. The town could not afford to mount the entire submarine in the park (now named Germanton Park), but built an area of sufficient size to make it look like the submarine had just surfaced in the grassy park. It remains very well tended and is very impressive as a memorial.

Sydney was next! Sadly, for the first time on our long trip we had a poor hotel. It was billed as a Best Western so we expected it to be OK, but it was old, not as clean as we would have liked, and it seemed a bit rundown. Had it been anywhere else I would have rejected it, but we were due to fly out to Cairns in three days and we didn't have time to cast around to find a better hotel. We wanted to look around.

Sydney was fascinating and full of things to see and do. We took a tram into the centre and then walked through the Rocks, a district known for small streets and interesting pubs and eating houses. From there we walked up to the Sydney Harbour Bridge. We decided that neither of us was fit enough to climb up over the bridge so we had an ice cream and then took a harbour cruise which was outstanding. We followed that with lunch at a harbourside restaurant in one of market areas below the bridge. After lunch, we visited the Circular Quay area and the Sydney Opera House.

We had seen so many pictures of all those famous sights, but to actually be there was fantastic. Strangely enough, for me one of the highlights was the magnificent Royal Botanic Gardens, and also seeing the sandstone shell known as Mrs MacQuarie's Chair, named after the wife of the first governor of Australia. It is said that Mrs MacQuarie loved sitting there and looking out over Sydney Bay.

There was so much to see in Sydney that the time passed too quickly. I had not expected to see so many sacred Ibis birds calmly walking about in most of the public areas. They were clearly at ease with people and not in the slightest afraid.

We had a great time in Sydney and there is no doubt that we could easily have spent longer there, but a key part of our planning for the trip was that we wanted to see the Great Barrier Reef and the Queensland rainforest. To do that we planned to fly to Cairns where we could achieve both aims. However, there was now a serious hitch. A cyclone had struck the northern Queensland area and all flights into Cairns had been suspended. So we managed to spend another two days in Sydney before catching the first flight into Cairns after the devastating storm.

Neither of us were prepared for the devastation that we witnessed on getting off the aircraft in Cairns. A number of trees were down in the airport car park and several cars were crushed, high-sided vans had been blown over and many buildings had lost roofs. We caught a bus from the airport to our hotel, just off the waterfront in Cairns, and the scenes of devastation continued all along the route that we took. However, it was equally clear that this sort of event was not the first time that a cyclone had struck, and there were already large numbers of emergency services workers engaged in clearing up the debris.

We were scheduled to spend five days in Cairns and by our second day most of the area around the town centre was already cleared.

We took a day cruise on a large catamaran, out to a huge raft moored above a section of the Great Barrier Reef. From there we could take a swim using snorkels and flippers, looking at the colourful coral and fishes just below the surface. It was a magical experience. We also took a trip on a passenger submarine, fitted with observation windows in the hull. From there we could observe deeper parts of the reef and watch swimmers using scuba breathing apparatus in order to get deeper than we had been able to.

On our last day at Cairns we boarded a narrow gauge train to take a very scenic ride up into the high rainforest area north of Cairns to Karunda. Once again, this visit was wonderful, even though it was very wet. The rainforest was certainly living up to its name!

Karunda itself was very interesting, with many exhibitions and displays showing how the Aboriginal people lived and developed in the area, which remains a sacred site for them.

Finally, we took a wonderful cable car ride in a glass gondola over the forest canopy, back to the railway station for the return journey to Cairns. It was almost the end of our month-long tour of Australia. We flew to Brisbane the next day ready for our onward flight to Hong Kong.

Brisbane was a great two-day adventure and we loved riding on their mass transit 'City Cat' river taxis. These were large and very powerful catamarans which plied up and down the Brisbane river in much the same way as most cities use buses and trams. They were really fun and very cheap to use.

But all too soon it was time to climb aboard another jet plane for the long flight to Hong Kong.

We had not planned to remain in Hong Kong for very long, it was really only a short break in the long journey home. We were to have one full day and two evenings in the now Chinese-owned port and city. I had last visited about 20 years previously and was interested to see what had changed. All of the main sites, such as the Peak and its tram, were very much as I remembered them, but both Kowloon and the main commercial district had become much more heavily developed with new buildings and skyscrapers everywhere. It had also got far more expensive in almost every commodity. It was certainly no longer possible to pick up very cheap clothing as had once been the case. We did enjoy the Star Ferry, crossing several times between Hong Kong Island and the mainland commercial shopping areas.

Perhaps we had grown used to the open spaces of Australia and New Zealand because neither Paula or I particularly enjoyed our short visit to Hong Kong. It was just too crowded and noisy for us to enjoy it much.

The final part of our long around the world adventure was upon us and indeed the pressure was on because we had an urgent appointment as soon as we got home.

Our son Jeremy (Jez) had joined the RAF just as I was retiring from the police. He had graduated from his initial NCOs course at RAF Cranwell and had then gone on to RAF Shawbury in Shropshire, to complete his training as a qualified rotary wing air loadmaster. He was due to graduate from the important course at 10.30 am on the day that we were due to land back at Heathrow at 6.30. The timing was going to be tight! With that in mind, I had written to British Airways explaining the situation. I suggested that the key to a successful rapid departure from Heathrow was the recovery of our luggage and asked if it could be loaded with the first-class baggage which I knew was unloaded first. They replied sympathetically saying that they would see what could be done.

We reported to the BA check-in desk at the new Chek Lap Kok International Airport to be told, "Oh dear, it's not your lucky day!

We had been instructed to upgrade you to first class as well as your luggage, but as we are completely full we cannot do that, but we will try to give you a special treat back in the economy cabin." So our baggage was going first class but we were flying economy. Nevertheless, we were treated to a very nice bottle of champagne and an enhanced menu in economy. Other passengers must have wondered what was going on.

We arrived at Heathrow spot on time and, as arranged, our luggage was almost the first off the plane. We were met by our two daughters, Julie and Esme, and were quickly on the road to Shawbury, arriving in good time to take our seats for the graduation ceremony. We were all immensely proud to see Jez wearing his RAF brevet with the letters LM below. He was now a qualified rotary wing air loadmaster. He had been immediately posted to RAF Aldergrove Northern Ireland on the puma helicopter. We had a great celebratory evening at Shawbury and then booked into yet another hotel for the night before setting off home for the first time since mid January.

Brian Allinson as Chair of Council, with Paula

18

Back to work

For me, the great adventure was over and it was time to resume my police liaison duties for McAlpine helicopters. My round of visits to nearly all of the police air support units in the United Kingdom resumed, and now McAlpines was requesting my assistance at several aviation exhibitions where their aircraft were being shown. These now included European venues, such as in the Hague and at the Paris Airshow, where I was required to give presentations on the work of UK police air units.

One of my early tasks was to visit Eurocopter's HQ in Donauworth, just north of Munich in Germany. It was a fascinating experience and I was able to view the entire production facility and also visit two police ASUs in Bavaria.

Then, in early 2005, there came a new challenge and a completely new experience. The phone call came one Monday morning and the message from Eurocopter was, "Can you be in Beijing next Monday?" I was apparently required to give two separate half-hour presentations to Chinese police audiences on the use of the helicopter by the police in the UK. The 2008 Olympics were being planned and the Chinese police had recognised that they would need to make use of helicopters during that event. I was to assist in this.

But as usual, as a consultant and not an employee of Eurocopter, I was expected to get myself to Beijing ready to meet local Eurocopter agents on arrival. I needed to book my flights and to obtain a visa in order to visit China. In my case, the obtaining of the visa had been made simpler, because as I was providing a service at the request of the Chinese government they had provided me with a letter of support to hand to the visa office at the Chinese Embassy in London. I travelled to London on the Thursday, arriving at the Embassy at the appointed time, 10.30 am, and was then told to return at 2.30 pm when the visa would be ready. Booking the flight to Beijing was much more difficult than I expected. All direct flights were fully booked but I managed to get a flight on Thai Airlines to Bangkok where, after a five-hour layover, I got a connecting flight to Beijing. I will never forget the announcement on the aircraft tannoy as we were on final approach to Beijing warning passengers not to take photographs out of the aircraft windows as that could be regarded as spying! What was I getting into?

I was met by two representatives of Eurocopter China and driven to the luxurious KunLun Hotel on one of the outer rings of the Beijing circulatory road system. The hotel was very tall, circular in shape and beautifully fitted and staffed. There were at least three different style restaurants on the ground floor and a spectacular rotating restaurant at the very topmost floor giving constantly changing views of the Beijing skyline. I was a little concerned, though, for I was booked into the hotel for a full week and was expected to pay on my departure. By now I had a company credit card, but had only ever used it for staying at inexpensive Premier Inn-style hotels in England for one night. This was in a different league and I was quite worried about ending up in a Chinese gaol. In the end, I sent an email to Eurocopter telling them of my concern and was relieved to get a "don't worry" reply. It certainly was luxurious!

In the event, my presentation at a university campus in Beijing seemed to go very well and I had lots and lots of intelligent and searching questions from the 150 senior police officers present. To my amusement, however, it became clear that they found it very difficult, indeed almost impossible, to understand how, in our system, the decision to accept a task and to deploy the helicopter in response would be taken by the duty crew, who would normally comprise of two fully trained and experienced constables and a civilian pilot. It was quite clear from their remarks in response to my lecture that in China at that time, the decision to deploy would have to be made by someone of at least colonel rank, and even then after holding a meeting. The concept of rapid deployment was clearly not understood and was going to take a lot of explaining!

I was booked to give two such lectures in Beijing one week apart, and then a third in Shanghai. My time between the lectures was entirely free and the local Eurocopter office had arranged for me to be taken to several famous tourist locations which I much appreciated. I was able to visit Tiananmen Square, the Forbidden City, the Summer Palace and the Great Wall of China. It was wonderful. I was accompanied everywhere by a female guide who was very helpful and a male 'minder' who I suspected was supplied by the government to ensure that I didn't get into any trouble. I remember walking across Tiananmen Square one day and on looking up to the sky I remarked that I had never seen any aeroplanes. His response was to say that no aircraft were allowed to fly over the city because they might contain spies. I then said, "Well, of course that won't apply to the police, will it?" He said, "No, they can't fly over either." I said, "If that is the case, why on earth have I been asked to come here?" He shrugged and then said words to the effect that the chairman had decreed that the games must be a success so he supposed that some things might have to change! It later transpired that the government had instructed that police aircraft could fly over the city but to ensure proper security they would have to be flown by military pilots, not professional civilian pilots as we expected.

The second lecture in Beijing also went well and appeared to be appreciated by a number of senior officers, and then it was time to catch an internal flight to Shanghai for the third booking. I was not prepared for the huge high-rise development of the city itself. It all appeared very new and very impressive too, although interspersed amongst the modern skyscrapers were numerous beautiful traditional Chinese pagodas and decorative ponds full of fish.

However, my overriding memory must be of the famous 'Bund' beside the wide Huangpu River. The river itself is very wide and carries all manner of waterborne traffic.

On the far side of the river stands the magnificent Shanghai Tower. The night-time views of the Bund area is something I will never forget.

I was booked to return to the UK from Shanghai Pudong Airport and took the frighteningly fast Mag Lev train to the airport. I seemed to arrive almost before I settled into my seat.

The long flight home was again via Bangkok as there were no seats available on direct flights. Clearly China is rapidly becoming an important business centre.

On my return, I was required to brief Eurocopter regarding my findings and then rapidly returned to my liaison visits to UK police aviation units. By now, most units were modernising rapidly, helped by an ambitious financing programme aided by the Home Office. There were still really only two aircraft in contention, the McDonnell MD 902 and the Eurocopter EC135. However, the MD 902 was clearly in trouble. It was a fine pilot's aircraft, and it was clear that those pilots flying the 902 really liked it. The police observers also praised it but agreed that the visibility forward for the rear observer was restricted. But its Achilles heel was a poor and growing reputation for poor reliability and an even poorer reputation for replacement parts when needed. The MD factory was cash limited and the otherwise fine aircraft was suffering from a serious lack of support and development.

But our aircraft, the EC135, was not without its faults either. In its early form it had a limited payload, this was later improved in stages, but for a while one annoying fault became all too prevalent. The EC135, like all police aircraft, was powered by two jet turbine engines, either manufactured by the French Turbomeca company or the American Pratt & Whitney company. Both engines offered very similar performance and efficiency and their selection was very much a matter for the customer when placing an order for their machine. However, the engine and transmission were mounted onto the aircraft fuselage via flexible suspension bearers known as 'Arris pots'. In the early days of the development of the EC135 these Arris pots were failing with monotonous regularity.

The failure usually occurred in flight and was accompanied by a noisy and rough ride in the aircraft. Eurocopter tried very hard to redesign the pots but it took far too long to trace the design fault and bring about a lasting reliable fix. Police aircraft have to be able to respond to emergency calls at very short notice and by the very nature of their tasking are often flown at the limit of their performance. It followed then that our police customers were suffering a higher Arris pot failure rate than our corporate customers. My liaison visits were vital at that time to reassure our customers.

Eurocopter (now Airbus helicopters) were in a far better financial position than our rivals MD, and were able to concentrate all their efforts in resolving the problem. Very quickly, the EC135 built for itself a strong reputation for reliability and effectiveness. Sadly, in some ways that reflected adversely on the MD 902 which quite quickly began to lose out to the 135. I say sadly, because I always believed it was important for the service to have a choice of aircraft. It was good to have completion.

I was spending an increasing amount of time with the Police Service Northern Ireland (PSNI), encouraging them to supplement their initial fixed-wing aircraft, the Britten Norman Islander, by adding an EC135 to their fleet which they eventually decided to do. Indeed, the development was so effective that they soon decided to also purchase the EC135's bigger brother the EC145!

By now I was lecturing quite often in Europe, at the Paris Airshow in 2006, and at a conference in the Hague the same year. Then I received another request to return to China, this time to an important selection conference in the important city of Hangzhou. This was crunch time – the Chinese were about to make a decision as to what aircraft they were going to buy to use in the 2008 Olympic Games! A very high delegation of Eurocopter sales staff were going to Hangzhou to manage the negotiations, in competition with teams from Bell, MD and Agusta, the Italian helicopter manufacturer. Eurocopter had requested my assistance with their presentation.

But on our arrival it quickly became obvious that we were not going to be playing on a level playing field. We had all originally been told to prepare a 45-minute presentation of our product. But suddenly in our case and that of Bell and MD, the time for the presentation had been reduced to 30 minutes. Agusta's, on the other hand, had been increased to one hour! Our protests went unheard and it quickly became obvious that we were wasting our time.

To make matters worse, I could not fly home immediately as there were no suitable flights. So I resolved to explore Hangzhou, which I had been told was beautiful. However, my frustration was to get even worse as a thick fog rolled in and I was literally unable to see the beautiful central lake which the city is famous for.

Back at home, I continued my close contact with all UK police air units, but was also becoming increasingly involved in local government matters. I had been elected as a parish councillor in 2001 and, although it was initially at very low level, I was enjoying the ability to make a bit of a difference in deciding local issues. Then in early 2003 the local Conservative Party asked me to stand for election as their candidate for the South Gloucestershire District Council. It seemed to go very well for me and I easily topped the poll in the May elections and was appointed as one of the councillors for Stoke Gifford. There then followed four years of membership of the Planning and Transport committee and also the Health Scrutiny committee responsible for examining our health performance etc. It was very interesting indeed.

I was re-elected with an increased majority in 2007 and to my surprise was appointed as the cabinet member responsible for Planning and Transport and the Strategic Environment. It was now getting very busy, but I was still able to continue with my aviation consultancy. Probably because of my policing background, I was taking a close interest in transport matters and quite quickly was appointed to be chair of the Joint Transport Executive Committee of the four West of England local authorities. Now life was getting very busy indeed.

On the aviation front, darker clouds were gathering. Austerity had become the government watch word. It was clear that the cost of police aviation was becoming an issue. Politicians were losing interest in police efficiency, their determination to cut police budgets was becoming ever more apparent.

I had long been advocating the creation of a National Police Air Wing in order to increase efficiency in training, and through economies of scale in the bulk purchasing of fuel, insurance and maintenance contracts, etc. And at first it appeared that the government, through the Home Office, were indeed proposing to create a single National Police Air Service. However, as time went on, it became increasingly obvious that the name of the game was not about increasing effectiveness, it was purely that of dramatically cutting the cost of air support by reducing both the fleet and the number of bases by about 50%.

It was clear that UK Police Air Support, a service which by 2008 had led the world, was going to be reduced to a mere shadow of what it once was. I was determined to speak out about the folly of what was to happen and took every opportunity to explain what was about to happen to the service I was so proud of.

One day in early 2011, I was talking to my local MP who I knew well, and took the opportunity to tell him about my fears for the service. He informed me that he would be speaking to the Home Secretary Theresa May in a few days, and suggested that I should prepare a briefing note for him which I was pleased to do.

Within a relatively short period of time, about three weeks later, I was requested to call at the Eurocopter UK headquarters in Kidlington where I was instructed to report to my two managers. I was informed that they had received a visit from the new head of the National Police Air Service (NPAS) who was in possession of my briefing note to my MP. I was of course unaware of what he had said to my Eurocopter bosses, but they were clearly not at all happy with my actions and I was told that my services as a consultant were no longer required.

I was obviously not at all pleased by that decision, but recognised that they were in business to sell helicopters, and hoped to continue to do so after the creation of NPAS. My role was coming to an end anyway because once the National Air Wing became a reality purchasing would be done centrally. It was ironic in a way that the national service that I had long argued for would be the reason my second career ended so suddenly.

The concept of NPAS was without doubt the way forward, and I remained in full support of the idea. What was so wrong was the manner in which NPAS was formulated, not to increase efficiency, not to improve value for money and effectiveness, but purely to save money. The huge reductions in fleet and bases meant that the remaining aircraft had to fly further and almost always arrived too late to be of any assistance. The criminals were now once again able to continue with their unlawful activities without the fear of being tracked from the air and arrested. Vehicle crime rapidly returned to the levels not experienced since forces obtained air support in the 90s.

I take no pride in saying it, but it is true that all the predictions that I made in that briefing note in 2011 have since come true. UK Police Air Support today is a sad shadow of what it once was. No new police helicopters have been purchased since NPAS took over. The fleet is now below 50% of what it was.

Sadly politicians have never quite grasped the fact that society is not inherently peaceable and honest. And in order for people to co-exist, there simply has to be law and order, and the law has to be enforced by an efficient and properly maintained police service. However, when society becomes calm and ordered, they assume that they can save money by cutting police budgets. That is a serious mistake. The calmness in society is merely an indication that you have the level of policing about right. It is not wise to use that as an excuse to save money!

Paula and I were continuing to pursue our main leisure activity of long-distance caravan touring, usually in France, and in 2015 decided to head for a small caravan and camping site at Meze on the Mediterranean coast near Sete. It was a long and hot drive requiring two overnight stops en route but late on a Friday evening in late August we arrived at Meze, booked in and were allocated a pitch beside the huge coastal lake, the Etang de Thau.

Being very tired after the journey, we slept well and did not rise quite as early as usual but at about 9 am I was awoken by the constant sound of emergency two-tone horns. I left the caravan and walked up to the site entrance and spotted in the distance, some way inland, a very big cloud of light coloured smoke rising some distance into the sky. This was obviously the cause of the emergency horns.

It was seemingly some miles away so I was not too alarmed and returned to the caravan for breakfast. But by 10 am the alarms were getting even stronger and I began to feel uneasy, so once again returned to the entrance of the site.

By now the fire was much closer and I could see huge walls of flame climbing into the air. Worse still was the fact that there was now a huge traffic jam blocking the road past the site.

There were literally 20 to 30 small fire engines interspersed with hundreds of cars. None of them were able to move, and it was immediately clear that there was now no possibility of escape even if we wanted to. Whilst somewhat alarmed, I was reassured in the knowledge that if the worse came to the worse we could always wade out into the Etang and should be relatively safe.

Then I heard the sound of approaching Aero engines, and suddenly there appeared a flying circus ring of 12 twin-engined red and yellow-painted Caribou aircraft, flying southwards over the Etang, and then turning directly towards us, landing at speed onto the water, filling their water tanks and lifting off again, flying directly over us, dropping the water from their tanks onto the brush fires behind us. This flying circus continued until mid afternoon when they managed to extinguish the fires! I got very wet taking lots of photographs. We will never forget that experience!

Apart from our adventure on arrival, the ten days that we spent in that region around Sete was stupendous. I have always loved sea food, and of course the Etang de Thau is famous for its sea food farms. The Etang is home to many farms specialising in raising oysters and mussels. There are also several small fishing ports located around the basin.

The region is a truly wonderful part of the southern coast of France, however unlike the more well-known areas such as Marseilles and Antibes, it is not outrageously expensive!

I redoubled my interests in local politics and continued as the local district councillor for Stoke Gifford. I was again successful at local elections in 2011, 2015 and 2019. I am resolved not to stand again in 2023 because I will have served for 20 years as a district councillor and that, together with my 30 years as a police officer, will mean 50 years in public service. I think that that is probably enough!

In 2019 I was given the huge honour of being appointed chairman of South Gloucestershire District Council. No member of my family as far as I am aware has ever done anything similar. I thank my long-suffering wife Paula and my children Julie, Jeremy (Jez) and Esme for putting up with all my moves over the years, and for always supporting me. I am so proud to have seven wonderful grandchildren Naomi, Tom, twins Imogen and Leo, Lennie, Lexie and Woody!